RIGOR, RELEVANCE, AND RELATIONSHIPS

IN ACTION

INNOVATIVE LEADERSHIP *and* BEST PRACTICES *for* RAPID SCHOOL IMPROVEMENT

WILLARD R. DAGGETT

Copyright © 2015 by International Center for Leadership in Education, Inc.
All rights reserved.
Published by International Center for Leadership in Education, Inc.
Printed in the U.S.A.

ISBN-13: 978-0-545-90796-5
ISBN-10: 0-545-90796-9

International Center for Leadership in Education, Inc.
1587 Route 146
Rexford, New York 12148
(518) 399-2776
fax (518) 399-7607
www.LeaderEd.com
info@LeaderEd.com

Dedication

The teaching profession is becoming more and more stressful and demanding. I am increasingly concerned for and respectful of our teachers.

My children and now my grandchildren have been blessed to have many extraordinary teachers. I dedicate this book to those teachers and all of their colleagues across this great nation.

Contents

Acknowledgments ix

Prologue xiii

Introduction 1

Part One: Taking Stock: Where We Are and Where We Need to Go 5

Chapter One: How Are We Doing? 7

Chapter Two: What's Our Purpose? 15

Chapter Three: Take Control, Don't Be Controlled 21

**Part Two: The Daggett System for Effective Instruction:
A Framework for Taking Control** 35

Chapter Four: It Takes Everyone 37

Chapter Five: How Do We Get Started? 47

Chapter Six: A Closer Look: Organizational Leadership 59

Chapter Seven: A Closer Look: Instructional Leadership 77

Chapter Eight: A Closer Look: Teaching 93

**Part Three: The Daggett System for Effective Instruction:
Best Practices** 107

Best Practices: An Overview and DSEI Alignment Reference Charts 109

Chapter Nine: Organizational Leadership Best Practices 115

    1. Why Not Us? 116

    2. Attaining Excellent Achievement Through Strong
       School Culture 118

3. Creating a Vision Where Teachers and Staff Lead
by Example 122

4. Fiscal Responsibility to Student Achievement 124

5. Twenty-First Century Learning Spaces 126

6. 3-D "Virtual Classrooms". 128

7. Empowering Teachers to Lead 130

8. Aligning Evaluation with Teacher Support............... 133

9. Districtwide Data Newsletter 137

Chapter Ten: Instructional Leadership Best Practices 141

1. Creating an Inspiring Vision and Culture of
"No Excuses" Teamwork............................... 142

2. Literacy for All, No Exceptions 145

3. Teaching Digital Literacy and Citizenship Skills 152

4. The Independent OpenCourseWare Study (IOCS) Program .. 155

5. Making Student Thinking Visible—Reflective Writing
Across Content 160

6. Assigning an Integration Curriculum Specialist 163

7. Close Reading in the Secondary Classroom 165

8. Measuring Perceptions of Rigor, Relevance, Relationships,
and Leadership in a School 172

9. Student Literacy Growth Profile 174

10. Data-in-a-Day 177

11. Worlds of Learning @ NMHS: Digital Badges in
Professional Learning 178

12. Principal Professional Learning Communities 181

13. Focus on Digital Learning Environments 183

14. Equity Through Family Engagement: The King Project 185

Chapter Eleven: Teaching Best Practices 189

  1. Developing a Product or Service: From Concept to Reality . . . 190

  2. Early Career Awareness: Linking Lessons to Career Skills . . . 192

  3. Creating Real Job Opportunities in the School 194

  4. Who Do We and Don't We Know? 196

  5. Building Relationships Through Culturally Responsive
     Activities 198

  6. Flipped Classroom 200

  7. Developing Content Knowledge with Graphs and Charts
     Across the Curriculum 203

  8. Leveraging Technology to Teach Self-Directed
     Learning Skills 213

  9. Book Buddies 216

 10. Game-Based Learning in the Classroom 218

 11. Technology Integration Through *Julius Caesar* 220

 12. Formative Assessment: The Exit Ticket 222

 13. Electronic Portfolio of Student Work 224

 14. Focused Differentiated Instruction 227

 15. Literacy Workshops to Improve Literacy Across Subjects . . . 232

Epilogue **235**

Acknowledgments

This book is the result of a collective effort by a team of dedicated and competent professionals.

Leading that list is Tim Weller, who was my partner in conceptualizing the idea, interviewing the contributors, and creating the manuscript. As a former reporter and editor for *USA Today* and the *Detroit News*, his writing and editing skills have been invaluable to me.

Three additional individuals also deserve special acknowledgment for carrying the lion's share of moving this book from a concept to a finished product. They are our incredibly talented editor, Kelly Griego, who guided, directed, and edited our work to arrive at a finished product of which we are all proud; Jerry Pedinotti, who helped collect, review, and edit all of the best practices and was essential to the completion of the book; and Dr. Linda Lucey, Executive Director of Program Design at the International Center for Leadership in Education, who managed the many moving parts in putting this book together.

Dr. David Anthony, Dr. Susan Szachowicz, Dr. Gregg McGough, Sharon Wolder, and Dr. Carol Johnson, whose interviews are presented in the book, provided important perspectives for which we are most grateful.

To all of those dedicated professionals whose best practices comprise Part Three of the book, we wish to commend you. Thank you for your effort in devising these best practices in the name of student-centered teaching, and thank you for your willingness to share them with your colleagues in the profession. Our best practices contributors include:

- Paul Andersen, AP Biology Teacher, Bozeman High School, Bozeman, Mont.
- Dr. Kathy Attaway, Director of Professional Learning, International Center for Leadership in Education
- Marilyn Boerke, Principal, Liberty Middle School, Camas, Wash.
- Pam Boatright, Principal, Truman High School, Independence, Mo.
- Sarah Box, Principal, North Side Elementary School, Harrisburg, Penn.
- Andy Bristow, Principal, Simpson Middle School, Marietta, Ga.
- Dr. Luvelle Brown, Superintendent, Ithaca City School District, Ithaca, N.Y.
- James Bruni, Director of Curriculum & Technology, Seneca Falls Central School District, Seneca Falls, N.Y.
- Matthew E. Calderón, Superintendent, Pembroke Central School District, Corfu, N.Y.
- Rob Carroll, Principal, South Heights Elementary School, Henderson, Ky.
- Danielle Chapman, Instruction Support, Salmon River Middle School, Fort Covington, N.Y.
- Jo-Lynette Crayton, Executive Director for Elementary Schools, Killeen Independent School District, Killeen, Texas
- Dr. Ed Croom, Superintendent, Johnston County Schools, Smithfield, N.C.
- Tim Davey, Technology Instructor, Salmon River Middle School, Fort Covington, N.Y.
- Marcie Donaldson, 7th Grade Reading and Language Arts Teacher, Simpson Middle School, Marietta, Ga.

- Laura Fleming, Library Media Tech, Consultant and Creator of Digital Badge PD Platform, New Milford High School, New Milford, N.J.
- Sue Gendron, President, International Center for Leadership in Education
- Teresa L. Glavin, Instructional Support Services Director, Otsego Northern Catskills (ONC) BOCES, Grand Gorge, N.Y.
- Greg Green, Principal, Clintondale High School, Clinton Township, Mich.
- Jessica Groff, Teacher, New Milford High School, New Milford, N.J.
- Andrea Hogentogler, English Teacher, Central Dauphin High School, Harrisburg, Penn.
- Deborah Holmes, Consultant, International Center for Leadership in Education
- Beth Howell, Principal, Kathleen H. Wilbur Elementary School, Bear, Del.
- Diane Jones, Consultant, International Center for Leadership in Education
- Glenn Ledet, Senior Consultant, International Center for Leadership in Education
- Dana Lee, Consultant, International Center for Leadership in Education
- Carol Lopez, Principal, Chambers Hill Elementary School, Harrisburg, Penn.
- Dr. Gregg McGough, English Teacher, Penn Manor High School, Millersville, Penn.
- Dr. Patrick Michel, District Superintendent and Chief Operating Officer, Hamilton/Fulton/Montgomery BOCES, Johnstown, N.Y.
- Thomas Miller, Principal, Brooks-Quinn-Jones Elementary School, Nacogdoches, Texas
- Sheila Mitchell, Superintendent, Anderson County Schools, Lawrenceville, Ky.
- Dr. Michael Nagler, Superintendent of Schools, Mineola Union Free School District, Mineola, N.Y.

- Angela Robert, Director of Instruction, Salmon River Middle School, Fort Covington, N.Y.
- Tammy Russell, Principal, Salmon River Middle School, Fort Covington, N.Y.
- Eric Sheninger, Former Principal, New Milford High School, New Milford, N.J.
- Dr. Susan Szachowicz, Principal (Retired), Brockton High School, Brockton, Mass.
- Scott Traub, Executive Director, West Region, International Center for Leadership in Education
- Catherine Truitt, Consultant, International Center for Leadership in Education
- Beverly Velloff, Elementary Mathematics Coach, School District of University City, University City, Mo.
- Doug Walker, Senior Consultant, International Center for Leadership in Education
- Joanna Westbrook, Teacher, New Milford High School, New Milford, N.J.
- Erika Willis, Principal, E.H. Phillips Elementary School, Harrisburg, Penn.

And last, but certainly not least, to all the teachers and school and district administrators who are working selflessly and tirelessly to right the ship, to do their part in moving our entire education system into the twenty-first century to give our children the promise of hopeful and successful futures, you have my endless respect, gratitude, and admiration.

Prologue

The World We Live In

"Grandpa, please don't start," two of my teenaged grandchildren, Lauren and DeAnthony, both begged. During a recent visit with them, I began lecturing them on their "digital footprints." A digital footprint is exactly what it sounds like: a trail or "footprint" that people leave online. This might include an email, an attachment, a digital image, or any form of online communication.

Like their peers, both Lauren and DeAnthony, whom we call "De" for short, are what we at the International Center call "digital natives." They are completely at ease using the latest devices, software, and apps.

At one point Lauren asked me if I had heard of Snapchat. Actually, I had. Snapchat is a mobile app that allows users to send and receive photos and videos that ultimately vanish. The sender determines for how long, from one to 10 seconds, a viewer can see the file before it disappears.

Seems like the perfect defense against a digital footprint.

"Grandpa, the image goes away, it just goes away," Lauren told me in earnest.

But De was waiting to pounce. "Lauren, do you know about Snap-Hack?" he asked. "You know, with this app I can show Grandpa all of your Snapchats." Terrified, Lauren lunged at her cousin and grabbed the phone from his hand. She instantly understood that somehow, Snap-Hack could retrieve her disappearing Snapchat images.

"Actually, Grandpa," Lauren said sheepishly. "It sounds like it's more of a digital tattoo." Out of the mouths of babes.

Welcome to a brave new—and scary—digital world.

The Future Is Now: Have Schools Gotten the Memo?

Google won its first patent in 1998, but it wasn't until 2002 that it started generating some traction. Google was born during what was called Web 1.0. It was informational. If you wanted *information*, you used Google to find your answer. Web 2.0 is what we call *relational*. The relational web lets you interact with other people through applications like Facebook, Twitter, LinkedIn, Pinterest, and the like.

Web 3.0 is just beginning, but it will explode exponentially in the coming months and years. Web 3.0 is *anticipatory*. Many are already calling it the "anticipatory web."

The key characteristics of the anticipatory web are artificial intelligence and deep data mining. When you Google something, an advertisement pops up. Do you see the same advertisements I do? Probably not, because my Google searches are different from your Google searches. What's going on here is data mining. Google tracks what you've searched for and purchased. Algorithms analyze data and then push related ads or search results to you.

We've already become pretty familiar with this degree of anticipatory web. It might feel intrusive and annoying, but not necessarily alarming.

Or is it? Those of us who use Gmail, Google's email service, have probably noticed that Google pushes ads based on what we've typed in an email. It's also storing people we often email as a group and making suggestions accordingly if a person is omitted from a particular email. This doesn't apply just to Gmail; Yahoo also scans its users' emails for ad targeting. (Sullivan, 2013) And thousands of companies route their emails through Google's servers. (Epstein, 2013) Think Google isn't scanning and storing those emails? Think it will stop there? (Foremski, 2010)

Digital tracking isn't reserved just for things you do online. Do you have any loyalty or rewards cards from stores? Those cards are tools to track your shopping patterns so that retailers can market specifically to you. (Linkhorn, 2013) Okay, in and of itself, not so bad. But what if this data becomes available for sale? There is a class of jobs out there called "data brokers"—people who negotiate with companies to sell your data to other companies or agencies. (Beckett, 2014)

When an endless amount of data can inexpensively be stored in the "cloud," where will it end? Who else might get this information, and what are they going to do with it?

This should make you shudder as you contemplate the future.

In a year or two, but perhaps much sooner, just about anybody will be able to mine all sorts of data. You and I will be able to buy applications that capture information on just about anyone.

Don't believe me? It's already happening.

Consider human resources in virtually every major corporation, which are creating social media review departments. Colleges and universities have done the same. Why? Because they want to vet potential employees and students.

Think of the implications this has for our students. Might they not get into college? Might they be turned down for good jobs before even getting the chance to interview?

Think about the implications for us as educators. Imagine you irritate or anger someone, be it a parent, student, or colleague, and he or she wants to do a search on you to see what you're all about. Eventually, they will be able to utilize data mining services and learn the websites you've visited, what you've Googled, what you've written in emails and to whom.

Are you preparing your students for this world? Are you educating them about the implications and the permanence of the Internet? Are you teaching them to use technology wisely and effectively? Or, like too many educators, do you see the Internet as a distraction to learning and, thus, make your students power down their smart devices when they enter school and ignore the topic altogether?

The Missing Middle

Okay, so to get past the first significant hurdle to college acceptance or candidacy for the jobs of tomorrow, students must be aware of the "digital tattoo" they are creating today.

But then what?

Then they need the skills that tomorrow's jobs will require of them. Are we teaching students those skills?

From 1950 to 1970, median income for all workers showed a healthy and consistent uptick. (Greenstone and Looney, 2011) Thanks to new technologies and new overseas markets, the rising tide lifted most every ship during that period. By virtue of meteoric growth in job demand, millions of people without college degrees were bumped up into the expanding middle class.

Then around 1970, something happened. A large segment of men found themselves dropped from the virtuous cycle of economic expansion.

It was at this time that new technologies displaced entire categories of plant- and factory-based labor. Those workers—mostly men of limited or unspecialized skills—found themselves with stagnating wages as technology cheapened their skill value or, worse, left them without work. They were qualified for only a limited scope of jobs, and those jobs were disappearing. They had no choice but to take lower-skilled and lower-paying jobs. Since then, while GDP has been on an upward climb, average annual income for men has dropped nearly 30 percent, taking a chunk of the middle class along with it. (Greenstone and Looney, 2011)

But the damage didn't stop there. Remember when you used to call a travel agent to book a flight? Or go into the bank to have a teller withdraw funds from your account? When's the last time you used a phone book? How often do you check yourself in for a flight through an airport kiosk?

In the early twentieth century, the assembly line and mechanization wiped out low-skilled jobs. In the late twentieth century and early twenty-first century, advancements in automation and Internet technology came after middle-class jobs. And the damage still didn't stop there.

Robotics and artificial intelligence will replace yet more workers in the middle class. And slowly but surely, they are coming after certain segments of high-skilled labor. (Aquino, 2011)

There are currently a few drug stores in the country experimenting with robotic pharmacists. Not only is this a cost savings, but these robots also have a zero percent prescription error rate.

Believe it or not, lawyers, and certainly paralegals, may be the next automated. New software can review and analyze legal documents for a fraction of the cost. Why pay $500 per hour in legal fees when you can make a one-time software expense?

The Internet has brought newspapers to their knees. For years, we've been hearing about sweeping layoffs that newspapers have made in an attempt to survive. And now that there's software that can write straightforward news stories, for how much longer are papers going to pay to keep general reporters on staff?

Accounting as a profession will in effect be gone in a matter of years. Inexpensive software is rapidly replacing the need for human involvement in tax preparation.

Computers and robots do not need to be paid. They don't need health insurance. They don't get sick or take vacations. They make few mistakes. It's only inevitable that as automation technologies become more mainstream and affordable, companies will choose them for cost savings.

What does this mean? It means the middle will go missing. It's already happening. Consider this: half of the jobs knocked out in the Great Recession paid between $38,000 and $68,000 per year. (Condon and Wiseman, 2013) As of 2013 data, only about 2 percent of the jobs we've regained since 2009 pay in that range; about 70 percent pay below that range, and about 28 percent pay above it. (Condon and Wiseman, 2013)

The following chart speaks to these circumstances. It shows job share by job skill level from 1980 projected through 2040. Low-skilled jobs and high-skilled jobs are and will continue to increase; as a growing share of the country climbs in wealth, they will grow the demand for low-skilled services, like lawn care, cleaning services, and other help staff. Mid-level jobs will continue to vanish before our eyes. I call this the "missing middle."

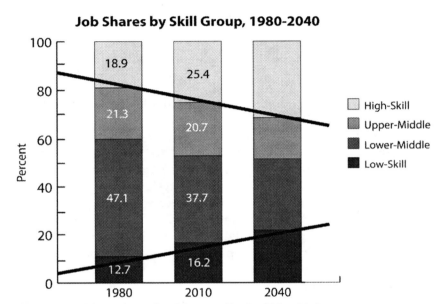

Job Shares by Skill Group, 1980-2040

Data sourced from the Federal Reserve Bank of New York and the U.S. Census Bureau.

While technology is encroaching on certain high-skilled jobs, it is creating new categories of technology-based high-skilled jobs. It's also creating a skills gap; several companies today cannot find enough people with the relevant skills to fill their high-skilled job openings. (Woellert, 2012)

Our education system no longer adequately prepares students for the career options they will face upon graduation. Students in our schools are, flatly, not getting the skills upgrade they need to land the high-skilled, well-paying careers of the future.

Can we, as educators, in good faith believe it's sufficient to prepare our students for the missing middle? We can't. Those jobs won't be there for our students when they graduate. We have to choose: prepare students for lower-skilled jobs or do the hard work and prepare them for high-skilled careers.

What do you choose?

The Future Is Now: This Is the Memo

I believe we have the best education system in the world. Through direct consulting and research or speaking engagements, I am acquainted with educators in every state. I have also spoken in 29 countries and observed just as many international school systems. Our system and our educators are superior; I have witnessed it repeatedly.

My wife Bonnie and I have five children, each at a different level of ability. Our children range from being gifted to having special needs. Two of our children have disabilities that required a very specific kind of learning and care. Each of our children found a school and academic program that not only fit his or her needs, but also allowed each to thrive and *improve*. Through our education system, each of our children excelled to his or her potential.

I can say it beyond a shadow of the doubt: no other education program in the world can accommodate the broad needs of my five children. We have the most open, accepting, flexible, and customizable education program in the world. We have highly competent and able educators within the system who, with great empathy, are ready to handle the needs of all students.

We should be very proud of this. *You* should be very proud of this.

But we do have our challenges. And we must be honest about them. The biggest threat to our educational excellence is the fact that we, as a system, have not updated our collective mindset to meet the needs of twenty-first century learning. The world is changing around us at a rapid pace. In general, schools are not keeping up.

What this means is that we are not preparing our students for the world and careers that await them. Think about this. Think about what this means—to their futures, to our country's future.

It is my belief that our shortcomings are largely the consequence of the outdated system we still work within. It must be updated and adapted to make space for productive and systemwide changes. We need to modernize what and how we teach. To do this, we have to modernize the entire system. And to do this, we have to *take* control—not *be* controlled.

The aim of this book is to help you—teacher, principal, school administrator, central office employee, superintendent—do just that. It *is* doable. We all have to be in it together.

References

Aquino, Judith, (2011). "The next 9 jobs that will be replaced by robots." Businessinsider.com: http://www.businessinsider.com/9-jobs-that-are-already-being-replaced-by-robots-2011-3?op=1, 17 March 2011. Retrieved 12 January 2015.

Beckett, Lois (2014). "Everything we know about what data brokers know about you." *ProPublica*: http://www.propublica.org/article/everything-we-know-about-what-data-brokers-know-about-you, 13 June 2014. Retrieved 14 December 2014.

Condon, Bernard and Paul Wiseman (2013). "Millions of middle-class jobs killed by machines in great recession's wake." Huffingtonpost. com: http://www.huffingtonpost.com/2013/01/23/middle-class-jobs-machines_n_2532639.html, 23 January 2013. Retrieved 17 February 2015.

Epstein, Robert (2013). "Google's gotcha: 15 ways Google monitors you." *U.S. News and World Report*: http://www.usnews.com/opinion/articles/2013/05/10/15-ways-google-monitors-you, 10 May 2013. Retrieved 14 December 2014.

Foremski, Tom (2010). "Google keeps your data forever—Unlocking the future transparency of your past." SiliconValleyWatcher.com: http://www.siliconvalleywatcher.com/mt/archives/2010/03/google_keeps_yo.php, 8 March 2010. Retrieved 17 February 2015.

Greenstone, Michael and Adam Looney (2011). "Trends: Reduced earnings for men in America." Brookings Institute (2011): http://www.brookings.edu/research/papers/2011/07/men-earnings-greenstone-looney. Retrieved 12 January 2015.

Linkhorn, Tyrell (2013). "Retailers use variety of ways to track consumer habits through loyalty programs." *The Blade*: http://www.toledoblade.com/Retail/2013/08/11/Retailers-use-variety-of-ways-to-track-consumer-habits-through-loyalty-programs.html, 11 August 2013. Retrieved 14 December 2014.

Sullivan, Danny. "As Yahoo begins scanning email to target ads, is it next on Microsoft's 'scroogled' list?" MarketingLand.com: http://marketingland.com/yahoo-email-scan-microsoft-scroogled-46416, 2 June 2013. Retrieved 14 December 2014.

Woellert, Lorraine. "Companies say 3 million unfilled positions in skill crisis: Jobs." *Bloomberg Business*: http://www.bloomberg.com/news/articles/2012-07-25/companies-say-3-million-unfilled-positions-in-skill-crisis-jobs, 25 July 2012. Retrieved 17 February 2015.

Introduction

This book is for those looking to do right by our students and deliver on our promise to prepare them for productive lives as adults in the twenty-first century. In other words, *this book is for all educators*. Throughout the book, you'll see mention of public schools. This is simply because most of the work we do and most of the research we have done pertains to the unique structure and challenges of the public school system. But this book applies to all Pre-K–12 schools.

If you are an educator living in our rapidly changing world, this book is for you. Public schools, private schools, charter schools, even parents who home school—we are *all* up against a swiftly changing economy and environment, and we *all* want our students and children to succeed now and in their futures. We *all* need to adapt how we think about teaching for the twenty-first century.

At the International Center, we are always being asked for more best practices. Demand for strategies and tactics to bring learning into the twenty-first century is high. This is a hopeful sign. We know intuitively and we know explicitly that things have to change. We reached out to our vast network of educators, administrators, and consultants to learn field-tested best practices. In this book, we've provided what we intend is a broad range of best practices that speak to everyone in the education system and vary in degree of complexity. But just because we had to hit print on this book does not mean we will stop collecting best practices. We are committed to doing what we can to help make the entire system student-centered. Check back with us at the International Center for new best practices.

When I set out to write this book, I knew I could not just list best practices in a vacuum. From my more than forty years in education—from the classroom, to the state office, to the International Center—I know that a smattering of best practices isn't enough. Best practices are critical to successful, student-centered learning. But they must be used within a larger vision and toward a clear objective.

To contextualize the best practices and provide them fertile ground for success, we've put them within the framework of the Daggett System for Effective Instruction, or DSEI. DSEI was born from this research-based realization: teachers are the most important players in student learning, but they cannot affect sustainable change alone. They need support from their school and their district. Everyone—*from the classroom to the boardroom*—must be aligned and working toward the same clear, definable, and measurable goal around student achievement. DSEI is a tool to do just that: help everyone in the system get on the same page, articulate a clear objective, and then measure each initiative, program, hire, structure, and decision against it.

Of course, student achievement is central to DSEI. And rigor, relevance, and relationships are the unequivocal and essential components of student achievement. The "3 Rs" serve as the guiding principles behind and backdrop to everything we at the International Center believe and do.

This book begins with an attempt to impress upon you the urgency behind our need for change. To support our larger aim, we use a combination of reports, studies, and our own experiential, observational research from working closely with districts, schools, and teachers for more than twenty years. At some points, you'll also notice I use strong language, sometimes even somewhat extreme. My point is neither to criticize nor generalize every teacher, every administrator, every school, or every district—I am aware of incredible strides being made across the country in the name of twenty-first century learning. We see exceptional, innovative instruction and leadership in model schools all the time and are proud of and heartened by the inspirational efforts of educators in every state. My focus here, though, is primarily on those districts and schools that, for whatever reason, remain stuck in the twentieth century. My language is strong to reflect the severity of the situation in schools where children aren't getting the tools they need for successful lives. Please read this book in the spirit it is intended: to drive the point home.

DSEI or otherwise, I hope to motivate you to discuss with your fellow educators devising some sort of plan to update and improve your school or district in the name of our students' futures. And, as you'll read, our country's future.

From there, we dig into DSEI, in what I intend as an approachable, easy-to-grasp way. For those of you who want to dig even deeper, in 2012 I wrote a book exclusively on the topic of DSEI, which is available online at store.leadered.com. But the aim of this book is to make DSEI less theoretical and more accessible, more anecdotal—*and more urgent.*

There are three main segments of DSEI: organizational leadership, instructional leadership, and teaching. Each segment has elements, or strategies, to bring effective change to each segment. Finally, we provide a series of best practices to implement each element.

This book is your guide to student-centered learning, your handbook in motivating your colleagues, your tool in mapping a plan, your source for best practices, your companion in making real, lasting change.

Are you ready? Good. Because now is the time. Our students are counting on us.

Let's get started.

Part One

Taking Stock: Where We Are and Where We Need to Go

Chapter One

How Are We Doing?

L et's get something straight right from the start: I believe our public education system is the best in the world. Period. I've spent my entire career in the field—as a high school teacher and coach, a state administrator, and founder and chairman of the International Center for Leadership in Education. I've traveled to all 50 states and to 29 different countries, and from what I've seen, our system, quite simply, is the best.

In the Prologue, I mentioned that my wife and I have five children, two of whom have special needs and required dedicated and individualized care while in school. In the United States, if a student has any form of disability, it is mandated that the student receive an Individualized Education Program (IEP). Within the IEP structure, teachers not only develop an instruction plan catering to the specific needs of each IEP student, but they also—and this is key—simultaneously look for opportunities for the student to access general curriculum. In other words, our system requires that we attempt to mainstream students with special needs. We are always looking for ways to loosen the restrictiveness of the learning environment for these students.

This does not happen in other countries. In most cases, other countries get overly caught up in the pursuit of excellence in education at the total expense of equity. When this happens, students with special needs are marginalized in society. In our country, we pull off the tricky balancing act between excellence and equity. As a result, we are preconditioned to believe that ALL students can achieve to their potential.

That said, do we apply this belief to ALL students with fidelity? We don't. Do we have the highest standards? We don't. Do we have the most relevant standards? We don't. Consequently, confidence in Pre-K–12 education, particularly in public schools, is starting to erode because we're just not preparing our students for the world in which they will live and work.

We find ourselves at a crossroads: improve our education system or risk becoming irrelevant to today's students as we fail to deliver on our promise to prepare them for a productive future.

It's been more than 30 years since President Reagan's National Commission on Excellence in Education released its landmark report, *A Nation at Risk: The Imperative for Educational Reform.* In short, the report claimed that the United States was failing to provide an education that would create a competitive workforce, with a potential for multiple dire effects over the long term. It made waves in 1983, and it still resonates today.

Since then, everything has changed—and nothing has changed. Take a look around you: what has changed? The world has changed! But education has not kept pace with that change. The purpose of education is to prepare kids for the future. Yet our focus is primarily preparing students for the next grade level. In doing so, we haven't adequately adjusted our goals to match the circumstances that have dramatically changed around us. Without noticing it, we as educators have become hung up on protecting the past, reinforcing a decaying, outdated system. By default, and in some cases by design, we are putting our interests—to maintain a system we're comfortable with—first instead of putting students' needs first. That's become our job.

In effect, schools today have become much like museums, where we spend each day figuring out where to move all our antique chairs and shelves. Unfortunately, that's what passes for reform. Today's schools, by and large, still run on an agrarian calendar. Today's schools, by and large, still operate on a bell schedule, a practice that dates back to the

Industrial Revolution. But the calendar says we're living in the twenty-first century.

Innovators and businesspeople are not only adapting to the ever-more technological and global world in which they work and live, they are also capitalizing on it. They are taking advantage of new technologies and the ability to connect with people all over the world to make their systems more efficient. Savvy businesspeople and innovators are always asking themselves, how can we improve the process? How can be more relevant and valuable to those we serve? They must ask these questions to survive.

Why don't we in education have the habit of always asking if we're still relevant and valuable to the students we serve? Why aren't we always updating the system to match the ever-evolving circumstances that surround us?

Uncle Sam Doesn't Want You

Let's dive a little deeper to illustrate the point.

A couple of years ago, I was invited to attend a forum where several governors representing the full political spectrum were brought together to see if they could find any common ground at all about Pre-K–12 education. They also brought in educators and business executives from across the country.

One of the speakers was Dr. Condoleezza Rice, who served as Secretary of State under President George W. Bush. No matter your stance on her politics or policies, she is a brilliant woman by any measure.

Today, Rice sits on the faculty at Stanford's Graduate School of Business and is a director of the school's Global Center for Business and the Economy.

I was puzzled. Why was she addressing this diverse group of governors, business executives, and other educators? What insights could she possibly bring to the table?

Now we know. Here's what she explained to the group:

For generations in this country, the military was the fallback plan for students who struggled in school.

That's not true today. Rice shared that at least 70 percent of all 17–24-year-olds are no longer eligible for the military, and we're headed to 80 percent within a decade.

How could this be possible? Here's how (Longley, 2009):

- About 25 percent of Americans today in the general 17–24 age group haven't graduated from high school. Today, if you don't earn a high school diploma, Uncle Sam doesn't want you.
- About 30 percent of those in this age group who do graduate from high school and want to join the military fail a mandatory admissions test focused on reading, writing, and math.
- Nearly 30 percent of Americans aged 17–24 are too overweight to join the military.
- And finally, about 32 percent in this age group have other disqualifying health problems, including asthma, poor eyesight or hearing problems, mental health issues, or recent treatment for ADHD.

"Imagine ten young people walking into a recruiter's office and seven of them getting turned away," former Undersecretary of the Army Joe Reeder said. "We cannot allow today's dropout crisis to become a national security crisis." (Longley, 2009)

Now let's look more closely at the military's admissions test.

The military calls the test ASVAB, which stands for the Armed Services Vocational Aptitude Battery. Recruiters and other officials give the test at more than 14,000 schools and Military Entrance Processing Stations around the country. The Department of Defense develops, administers, and—take note—updates the test every six months. Every six months!

The ASVAB is a timed multi-aptitude test that focuses on four critical areas: arithmetic, mathematics knowledge, word knowledge, and paragraph comprehension.

At www.military.com, the main online gateway for those considering military careers, the message is direct and hard-hitting: "If you're serious about joining the military, then get serious about ASVAB."

"Your scores…count toward your Armed Forces Qualifying Test (AFQT) score. The AFQT score determines **whether you're qualified to enlist in the U.S. military**" (emphasis added).

The website continues, "Your scores in the other areas of the ASVAB will determine how qualified you are for certain military occupational specialties and enlistment bonuses. A high score will improve your chances of getting the specialty/job and the signing bonus you want.

"Scoring high on the ASVAB will require study and concentration. Don't skimp on preparing for this test. **It's your future. Get the most out of it**" (emphasis added).

Clear and to the point, don't you think?

The businessfolks went ballistic after Rice's presentation. "If 70 percent of these young people are not qualified to join the military, what makes you think they are qualified to work for us?" they asked.

Indeed.

The World Is Changing Faster Than We Are

Why does the Department of Defense update ASVAB every six months? The answer is clear if you know even a little about today's modern military. Technology is critical to job performance. If you mess up in the military, someone might get hurt or killed. Military leaders understand they must constantly retrain their men and women as the standards change and the technology grows more sophisticated.

And here's the tie-in for us: if we don't deliver academics that are relevant and rigorous, then those students will not be trainable. Military technology—actually technology across the board—is getting more complex, which means the academic requirements behind them need to be more stringent. That's why the military so frequently updates and increases the rigor of ASVAB.

But We're Trying

Most sectors of society are adapting to our quickly changing world, or at least attempting to keep pace and take advantage of new opportunities. But we in education find it very difficult to initiate change in our schools.

Who said change is ever easy? It is hard, but what's the alternative? Do we just throw in the towel and keep pushing students along, year to year, grade to grade?

What happens when they leave school?

The Hard Truth

Consider again the reaction of those business executives to Rice's presentation: *if 70 percent of our kids are not prepared for the military, then what makes you think they are prepared for us?*

Exactly. Johnny or Susie may be academically qualified to work at a convenience mart, but they're certainly not ready to earn enough money to become self-sufficient. Think about what this means as a society, for our future. Will the number of Americans capable of being self-sufficient dwindle? Could 70–80 percent of our young people potentially be headed to public assistance? As a nation, that's unsustainable.

Other demographic indicators make matters worse.

Our aging population poses a problem. In the late 1950s and early 1960s, the United States had more people under 5 years old than over 55 years old. Not coincidently, this was the period when President Lyndon B. Johnson launched the Great Society program, expanding Social Security and creating Medicare and Medicaid. Unfortunately, everyone assumed the underlying demographics would stay the same, thus providing enough tax revenue to fund these programs in perpetuity.

Today, those numbers are reversed. Today, we've got more people 55 and older than we have under 21. And again, many in this latter group may be headed to public assistance.

I'll say it again: that is unsustainable.

When I address the business community and lay out the problem, their reaction is universal: "We have got to do something!" Educators respond by saying, "We're trying!"

The hard reality is—*trying* simply is not good enough. We don't have a problem in education. We have a crisis—and one that will ripple far and wide if not resolved. We did not create the crisis, but it is ours to solve.

If Not State Standards, Then What?

What I hear often from educators is that we're changing too fast—which brings us to the Common Core. As many of you know, 46 states initially adopted the Common Core State Standards, the goal of which is to better prepare students for college or a career. The Common Core establishes national standards, replacing state standards that varied from state to state.

The National Governors Association and the Council of Chief State School Officers developed the standards with help from teachers, parents, and other experts. Before Common Core, individual states decided what students needed to know. Under Common Core, a high school graduate from any state should, in theory, be ready for college or the workplace. Critics argue that decisions about education should be made locally and that the Common Core standards take away too much local control. Efforts to repeal or slow down Common Core have sprung up across the country. Some parents and teachers are howling because the tougher requirements mean they've seen their "A" students slip to "C" students and their "C" students slip to "D" or "F" students.

Here's the real issue: Common Core was written in 2008 and field-tested in 2010. Think about the mobile phone you used in 2008 or even 2010. Common Core is already outdated! So yes, changes in education are coming fast, but not fast enough.

I'm not here to support or oppose Common Core. I'm here to rally the troops to take control and bring the system into the twenty-first century. And I'm here to make you understand we don't have a choice. Schools are changing, but the world is changing faster than we are—four or five times faster. It was true in 1983 when *A Nation at Risk* was released, and it's even truer today.

We've talked about reform for the last 30 years, but little has changed. We keep drawing lines in the sand and then stepping back because "it's too hard." Sooner or later, we're going to hit the wall. And probably sooner.

So if not these standards, then what?

References

Longley, Robert (2009). "Up to 75 percent of US youth ineligible for military service." USGovInfo.About.com: http://usgovinfo.about.com/od/usmilitary/a/unabletoserve.htm, Retrieved 5 December 2014.

Chapter Two

What's Our Purpose?

Before I started the International Center for Leadership in Education in 1991, I worked for 17 years at the New York State Department of Education. For years, the department struggled to put into place what would today be considered minor educational reforms. Then in 1983, *A Nation at Risk* was released, sending shock waves across our landscape and touching off a surge of reform efforts.

The report noted that our educational system was failing to meet the needs of a competitive workforce. "The educational foundations of our society are presently being eroded by a rising tide of mediocrity that threatens our very future as a nation and a people," wrote J. Harvey, the report's lead author. "If an unfriendly foreign power had attempted to impose on America the mediocre educational performance that exists today, we might well have viewed it as an act of war."

The report showed that from 1963 to 1980, average SAT scores dropped more than 50 points in the verbal section and more than 40 points in the mathematics section. Nearly 40 percent of 17-year-olds could not successfully draw inferences from written material. Only 20 percent could write a persuasive essay. Only a third could solve a math problem requiring several steps. Comparing results to students in other countries, the report noted that in 19 separate tests, American students never finished first or second, but finished last seven times.

The commission recommended reforms in five major categories: content, standards and expectations, time, teaching, and leadership and fiscal support.

Motivated to Change

Perhaps because of my background in career and technical education the report resonated. I understood we needed to change, and quickly. That wasn't rocket science, of course—many educators knew what had to be done and how to do it. What *was* rocket science was how to actually move a bureaucracy. I was naïve enough to try—and promptly got the stuffing beat out of me by every special interest group around.

Our goal back then—as it remains today—was to help students develop the skills they would need to compete in a modern workforce. In New York, we decided to first target Industrial Arts and Home Economics, two courses that were failing to meet the needs of students growing up in the 1980s.

After much back and forth, we developed new courses to replace the shop course boys took and home economics course girls took. Two of the new courses, which ALL students would take, were called Principles of Technology and Home/Career Skills. The idea was to bring boys and girls together and teach them both sets of skills. We started working on this in 1983, and by 1985 the department made both courses a requirement in all 752 New York districts.

We designed the courses to:

- Increase the employability of students going from high school into the workforce.
- Emphasize the principles rather than the specifics of technology, as well as the underlying math associated with these principles.
- Maintain the academic rigor needed to meet the increased requirements in science for high school graduation.
- Have both boys and girls understand the importance of and develop skills to fulfill one's responsibilities in both home and careers.

We understood that we were living in a sophisticated, rapidly changing society dependent on an understanding of technology. The key was to develop a curriculum that not only taught employable skills, but also provided technical principles that would not become obsolete as equipment and technologies changed.

The business community loved it. Students were ecstatic. Teachers? Not so much. Several wanted my head. Despite the fact that the new courses were in the students' best interests, many educators preferred the status quo. The course pushed them out of their comfort zones. They didn't know how to begin to teach these concepts. No one knew what students needed to know, and no one knew what jobs were going to exist when these students graduated.

Eventually, we discovered the solution. We would need to constantly monitor the changing world and keep adapting what and how we taught based on what we saw in the pipeline. But what also became clear was that to deal with the uncertainty of the future, we had to teach students how to become lifelong learners.

Taking the Message on the Road

As a senior state executive, I often spoke with corporate leaders who hammered away at one message: "We're in deep trouble as a nation. You've got to start moving the education system."

Increasingly, various business and education groups asked me to speak. I continued to work for the state, but on weekends and vacations, I traveled around the country sounding the alarm: we've got to change, here's how we can change.

I started to wear down; I couldn't sustain the demands of the state job and this new, second career of frequently traveling to speak. I asked for and received a six-month leave. It was over that period that I decided to start my own education consulting company.

My colleagues thought I was crazy. I had a great job with security, a nice compensation package and phenomenal benefits. My wife, Bonnie, worked, but we also had five teenage children at home, two with special needs. What was I thinking?

Getting Help

I was thinking that this message was too crucial *not* to broadcast as far and wide as possible. But I couldn't do it alone. Early on, I reached out to my long-time assistant, Karen Wilkins. Karen and I first began working together in 1978 at the New York State Education Department and have remained a team since.

She continued working full-time at the Department of Education while I was on leave, but I asked her to help me out from time to time. In those early months, Karen worked with me on weekends and during her lunch hour. On her lunch break, she would leave her office, walk across the street and enter a nearby building that had a bank of pay phones on the first floor. From there, she would return calls to the various groups who wanted me to speak. Slowly, we began to build relationships with potential clients.

Calls came in on a telephone line we installed in the basement of Karen's home. We bought an answering machine and recorded a message that went something like this: "Hello, you've reached the International Center for Leadership in Education. We can't take your call right now, but if you leave us a message and a number where we can reach you, we'll return your call tomorrow between noon and 1 p.m." And like clockwork, the next day Karen would march across the street and start returning those calls.

It wasn't long before I asked Karen if she would join me full-time. This was asking a lot. She had a secure job and two young boys at home, but she took a gamble and joined me at the International Center.

I wasn't sure how I could pay her, let alone myself, in those early days. I just kept telling her, "Karen, you've got to trust me. I'll make things right." And I did.

Today Karen is my chief of staff. She knows more about our operations than I do.

Twenty-four years later, we've built an incredibly talented, dedicated and loyal staff and team of consultants that total more than 200. We are all united behind the same belief: *the purpose of education is to prepare students for the future.*

Chasing a Moving Target

Preparing students for the future is easier said than done; after all, the future is abstract and always changing. Doing so takes a commitment— to the practice of looking forward. Recall how the Department of Defense updates the ASVAB every six months to incorporate questions relevant to the most recent technological advancements in defense? Educators must adopt a similar practice.

Let me ask you this question: How many of you would let your students use their smartphones during a test? I'm betting your answer would be, "No!" Why not? "Because they'll cheat!" And how will they cheat? "They'll go online to find the answers, or they'll text each other to get the answers."

Let's look at this another way. If my grandmother were still alive today, she'd be more than 120 years old. She taught kids in a one-room school in northern New York State. When I first became a teacher, she told me a story that only now do I truly understand.

In the early part of the twentieth century, my grandmother—in fact, teachers in many schools—had something called a "pencil budget." This budget paid for pencils because schools didn't want students bringing their own pencils to school. Just imagine, if students brought pencils to school, they might write notes to each other. They might draw pictures. And if students brought pencils with erasers, they might change their answers on the daily quiz. The teacher could lose control of her class. So when a teacher wanted students to use pencils, she passed them out. When she finished the lesson, students returned the pencils.

When the Great Depression hit, administrators changed the rules. They realized that most students now owned their own pencils. So teachers took on a new responsibility—teaching students *how* to use their pencils responsibly.

Let me ask you that question again: Would you let your students use their smartphones during a test? "Of course not!" Why? "Because they'll cheat!" And how? "They'll go online to find the answers, or they'll text each other to get the answers!"

Would it be fair to say that those "cheating" students are using resources and learning to work with others? Would it be fair to say that they'd be looking for information the same way we, as adults in careers, do?

Do you have children living at home? Do you want them to develop into independent young men and women? What are the essential skills they need to become independent? Could the answer be "working with others and using resources effectively?"

The Waning Relevance of Schools

When we were children, we went to school because that's the place where we got information. If school was closed, we could go to the library to learn, or if our family was wealthy enough, we might have even owned a set of encyclopedias at home.

But today's students get their information 24/7 from their smartphones or tablets, which begs the question: what is the purpose of school today?

Today, hand-held technology is the pencil of my grandmother's era. Today, some teachers go crazy if students bring their phones or tablets to class. Why? Because it interferes with our twentieth-century, one-room schoolhouse educational model.

Today, our students literally hold the latest technology in their hands—but we won't let them use it because it intrudes on how we're used to teaching. To pretend we are going to win the battle against technology is to be as in denial as thinking pencils weren't a powerful tool for learning. Our students ARE going to keep using their technology devices. Shouldn't we be helping them learn how to use them effectively and wisely?

If the ultimate purpose of education is to prepare students for the future, how can that ever be possible if we as educators are teaching in the past?

Chapter 3

Take Control, Don't Be Controlled

At the International Center, we've found that the most successful schools have a different mindset from that of too many other schools. They are proactive—very proactive.

It's clear today that thousands of educators across the country are feeling close to burnout. They're overwhelmed by all the initiatives flying at them from every direction. This has forced them to be reactive, to base their school programs on what someone else is telling them to do right now.

I call this the "fog." Today's educators must somehow try to stay on top of all these new demands and still connect with each student in a meaningful and relevant way. Administrators must somehow keep outside forces satisfied and still support their schools and teachers. It's no wonder so many educators and administrators cannot find focus amidst the fog of external and conflicting demands.

Through our collaboration with the most rapidly improving schools, we see a recurring theme: these schools take control. They don't kowtow to the demands of outside influences because these educators understand something. They know that they have one job and one job only: to do what's best for students. Outside demands all too often come with motives that sideline teachers and students, and these schools simply won't allow teachers and students to be anything other than priority number one.

So where do they start? How do they pull this off? In the ensuing chapters, I will walk you through the Daggett System for Effective Instruction (DSEI), which provides a systemwide and holistic approach to reorienting the entire system toward student-centered learning and provides a framework for everyone in the system to remain in control of how students learn and why.

But there's something else that the most rapidly improving schools do with regularity and consistency. To proactively take control in the pursuit of student-centered learning, these schools first look down the road to see what's in the pipeline. After all, the ultimate aim of student-centered learning is to prepare students for the future. Therefore, we must somehow make a habit of anticipating what the future will hold. What are the major emerging trends? What's changing in technology and how we use it? What careers are consequently cropping up or dying off?

Identifying such trends is the first step to begin solving our problems. What's the point of teaching our students anything if they can't use what they learn in the world they'll face upon graduation?

Today's Five Emerging Trends

We at the International Center have identified five major trends having an impact on what and how teachers should be teaching today, and those trends follow. However, we practice what we preach: as we see the following trends become the norm or fall away, we will update them with what we see subsequently coming down the line.

What's in the pipeline today, as I write this book in 2015, that can be of use to educators committed to preparing today's students for tomorrow's world?

Emerging Trend #1: The Impact of Digital Learning

Today's learners are digital natives. Yet when they come to school, they power down their devices. As educators, we need to embrace the power of technology and work with it to make learning relevant for all students. Using technology effectively in everyday learning can help students strengthen their learning experiences and build on their intuitive technological skills. Using technology thoughtfully will allow us to stretch students' thinking in ways that will lead to success in our increasingly global economy.

Eric Sheninger, a senior fellow with the International Center and a leading authority on using technology to improve schools, puts it another way: "There's an automatic disconnect when kids go to school because they are entering a world that is opposite of the world they're immersed in."

We need to keep pace with students who operate in an increasingly mobile world. People access information and communicate using smartphones, tablets, and laptops. But too often, not in school. With more kids going mobile, social media provides the context for digital learners to connect, collaborate, and create content in ways that are especially meaningful to them. They use a wide range of tools to do just that, including these (Project Tomorrow, 2013):

- Texting: 71 percent of high school students and 63 percent of middle school students communicate through text messages, an increase of 44 percent since 2008.
- Twitter: Three out of 10 students in grades 6–12 use Twitter.
- Videos: The number of middle school students creating videos and posting them online has doubled from 15 percent in 2007 to 30 percent in 2014.
- Games: Nearly twice as many students in grades 6–8 participate in massive multiplayer online games compared with students in high school.

We believe a strong collaboration will develop between gaming companies and Pre-K–12 education publishers which will compete directly with the way we traditionally teach. Gaming companies have mastered the ability to engage students with highly individualized, user-controlled games. These games can provide immediate feedback and can be used any time, any place.

Sheninger agrees. "Gamification allows students to acquire and demonstrate special skills," he says. "You want to make learning fun. We need more examples of schools that are embracing game-based teaching and learning." (Sheninger, 2014)

Students will increasingly move toward these games, which will be more engaging and less expensive than our traditional educational model. But—and this is important—games lack the personal contact all of our students need. Strong teacher-student relationships help teachers make instruction relevant to their students. Relevance is highly personal; teachers must get to know all students to learn what is relevant and interesting to them. It takes relevance to make learning truly rigorous.

New Zealand Professor John Hattie's meta-analysis, described in *Visible Learning*, lists teacher-student relationships as one of the most effective influences on student achievement, outpacing professional development, teaching strategies, and socioeconomic status. (Hattie, 2009) Still, if educational publishers join forces with gaming organizations, I fear that many educators will see these products as so disruptive that they will treat games as the enemy. That is a battle we will lose. "We've got to help school leaders work smarter by harnessing and leveraging available technology so they can do what they do better," Sheninger says. "It's really about finding technology's natural, progressive fit into their core responsibilities." Schools that will flourish in this new world will be those that embrace digital learning and are willing to disrupt their traditional systems by creating a new hybrid. They will embrace the best of both systems.

We must ask ourselves: Are we asking technology to conform to our twentieth-century school practices? Or are we allowing technology to transform our schools into twenty-first century learning environments?

Emerging Trend #2: Heightened Demand for Career Readiness

It should be clear by now that preparing a young person for career success today requires a higher and different set of academic skills and knowledge than those taught in traditional schools. The workplace has fundamentally changed, and our education system has not kept pace. We are simply not preparing students for this changing work environment. Consider these facts:

1. The middle class is shrinking. Recall in the Prologue the chart about the missing middle? It's such an important point that it bears repeating. In the early twentieth century, technology replaced low-skilled labor. However, most people invested in education and upgraded their skills, positioning themselves to make significant gains during the post-World War II economic boom.

     Toward the end of the twentieth century, technology began knocking out mid-skilled labor. The difference in this case was that the rate of people investing in education stalled, and those who did turn to education were not guaranteed to get the skills they need for today's careers. (Greenstone and Looney, 2011) These people have fallen behind and stand little chance of catching up.

     The trouble didn't stop there. Technology continues to supplant even more mid-level jobs and it's hollowing out the middle class along with it; the middle has gone missing. While new technologies are beginning to encroach on high-skill jobs, it's also creating entirely new categories of jobs at the top.

Job Shares by Skill Group, 1980-2040

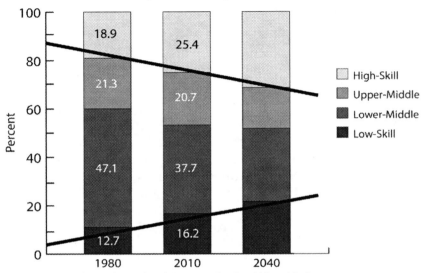

Data sourced from the Federal Reserve Bank of New York
and the U.S. Census Bureau.

To believe it's sufficient merely to prepare students for mid-level jobs is to believe in a future that won't exist. Those mid-level jobs are disappearing. The job options of the future will be more low-skill/low-wage jobs, more high-skill/high-paying careers, and far fewer middle-skill/middle-wage jobs. Our options as educators are to teach to the high-skilled jobs or, by default, relegate many students to a life of low-skill labor and no real chance for self-sufficiency.

2. In 2014, 40 percent of employers reported difficulty in filling job openings—despite the fact that around 13 million people are unemployed at any one time. (ManpowerGroup, 2014) Why? Employers say they can't find people with the necessary skills. This is commonly called the "skills gap."

3. There is a growing mismatch between college student majors and jobs. What a student majors in matters, and we're not telling them this. A U.S. Department of Education report found higher unemployment upon graduation among college graduates

who majored in general majors in liberal arts or humanities compared to those who majored in technical fields aligned with occupations, like health care or education, who experienced lower unemployment. (U.S. Department of Education, 2014) Higher education is not fundamentally changing to meet the fundamentally changing workplace

4. Forty-eight percent of employed, recent four-year college graduates are holding jobs that require less than a four-year degree. (Bidwell, 2013) Thirty-seven percent are in jobs that require less than a high school diploma. (Bidwell, 2013) For nearly 20 years, the increase in college tuition and fees has been twice the rate of inflation. The average student leaves college—whether or not he or she has earned a degree—with at least $36,000 in student debt. (Ellis, 2013)

5. Reading requirements for entry-level jobs are often higher than those needed for higher education.

Preparing our teachers to deliver the rigorous and relevant academics that will prepare students for college and career will require focused and sustained professional development, plus a number of fundamental shifts in how we organize the instructional programs in our schools. It will also require a conscious shift in our collective mindset away from protecting the existing system and toward fighting for the interests of our students.

Emerging Trend #3: Increased Emphasis on Application-Based Learning

Through our more than twenty years working with schools and districts across the nation, we know, believe, and have seen that relevance makes rigor possible. We also know that relevance does not occur one discipline at a time. For content to be relevant, the best-performing schools have found that students need to apply relevancy to their personal areas of interest. That is why the International Center's Rigor/Relevance Framework® has become the organizing framework for many schools as they implement new state standards and testing programs. By filtering standards through the Rigor/Relevance Framework, these schools remain in control of these outside demands, as they are making the standards fit their vision, rather than the other way around.

Today, "the facts" are everywhere and are widely available through a click of a mouse or a tap of a screen. "The facts" no longer need to be encapsulated, dispensed or acquired from an all-knowing source like a textbook, an encyclopedia, or yes, even a teacher. For many of today's students, the traditional classroom is an anachronistic model that simply doesn't relate to the world in which they live. They have figured out how to retrieve the information they need, how to use it to solve everyday problems, and how to communicate and collaborate with their peers about that same information. School seems increasingly disconnected from the very world for which we are supposed to prepare students.

Students will not learn unless they believe school is relevant. But here's the problem: what's relevant to one student is not relevant to the next. I've got a grandson who believes he's going to be a professional football player. I've got another who believes he's going to be a musician. They don't have any similar interests. Not one. However, can we teach math and science through football and use music and art to teach language arts? Yes! But you need an organizational structure to do that. The problem is we don't know how to organize our schools so we can use interests like football and music to teach math and science or language arts. Right now, we have just one way to organize schools. And when you think about it, there is no other industry on the face of the earth that believes what we believe—that every employee is at the same level. But we do. We believe every student is at the same level, and that's why our schools are organized the way they are. Doesn't it just seem ridiculous?

Some schools have seen the light and have moved to much more application-based instructional programs such as:

- Expeditionary Learning (EL), which is a model of education powered by a growth mindset. EL schools pledge to help students become "leaders of their own learning." EL is committed to "creating classrooms where teachers can fulfill their highest aspirations and where students can achieve more than they think possible." (Berger, 2013)

- Project-based learning implemented schoolwide. As an example, Decker Middle School in Austin, Texas, a member of the New Tech Network, engages all teachers in unit planning based on projects.
- Game-based learning emphasizes the principles of gaming—like micro-credentialing and digital badges, which are images or symbols that can be earned by meeting established performance criteria and that indicate the acquisition of specific skills or knowledge—in their daily curriculum. Game-based tactics work best when they are eased into classes or programs. This is because they are, frankly, controversial. They can be misperceived as playing. But when used appropriately, they enhance learning and serve as an excellent motivational tool. Importantly, they cannot be used to replace teaching: hands-on, relationship-based teaching must always remain the driving force behind twenty-first century learning. The point of gaming principles is to bring a fun, engaging element to class, not to displace teachers and the empowering human connection they can and must provide.
- The Rigor/Relevance Framework's Quadrant D learning, which is built around high rigor/high relevance learning. In schools that use this framework, such as Simpson Middle School in Marietta, Ga., the Rigor/Relevance Framework is the lens through which decisions around curriculum, instruction, and assessments are made. An important point to keep in mind about Quadrant D learning is that its aim is not to put all teaching in just that quadrant; it's merely to emphasize its need to be a consistent component of teaching, worked in as much as possible. But learning must take place in all four quadrants of the Rigor/Relevance Framework. To achieve this, high-level questioning, academic discussions, and authentic resources are integrated regularly.
- Industry certification and career academies, which can come in the form of a few courses or a "wall-to-wall" academy program, aim to arm students with relevant job skills, while simultaneously exposing them to a broad range of career tracks.

Academies are typically in partnership with local universities, government agencies, organizations, or businesses to collaborate in providing hands-on experiences that directly prepare students for jobs and careers. Programs can involve internships, networking opportunities, and industry certifications. In a wall-to-wall academy program, the traditional subject-driven paradigm is replaced by an exclusively academy-driven learning structure. This approach can be found at Clearwater High School in Clearwater, Fla.

Each of these application-driven programs provides a way for schools to ensure that curriculum and course content remain aligned to your vision and learning objectives and not diluted or overruled by outside demands. In any such paradigms that put learning in terms of their application, schools can remain in control.

Emerging Trend #4: Use of Data Analytics to Implement Growth Models

American education is overrun with research. Professor John Hattie analyzed 52,637 research reports on K–12 education—just since 2000. (Hattie, 2009) We have volumes of data, but we have not learned how to monitor, track, and introduce effective interventions based upon that data. What's clear is if we learn to use data with more sophistication, we will accelerate the movement toward implementing growth and continuous improvement models.

With more and more data on individual students, we will confirm what we intuitively know—that the one-size-fits-all approach to instruction does not work. Individualizing instruction will require focused and sustained professional development. It will also cause discomfort to those who wish to stay grounded in twentieth-century practices.

Data analytics will bring great opportunity and great challenges. Our present system focuses on tests that measure a student's degree of mastery of a set of knowledge at a given point in time. It does not typically focus on a student's ongoing growth and learning over time. That is about to change. By leveraging data and applying shrewd analysis, rapidly improving schools have been able to change their focus to a continuous improvement model for every student. Students are, in effect, evaluated by their progress, not by a test score.

The Literacy Growth Profile (LGP) is one analytics tool to do just that—measure a student's reading ability over time. Based on the Lexile® Framework for Reading, LGP also provides snapshot data that can indicate a student's level of preparedness to comprehend reading materials from a range of environments, such as high school, the military, entry-level jobs, and everyday personal use. LGP is a best practice used in the Hamilton/Fulton/Montgomery BOCES in Johnstown, N.Y.

Emerging Trend #5: Developing Personal Skills

How many of you have sons or daughters in their twenties? Are they bringing home a "significant other" more frequently? When you realize that this person may one day be your future daughter- or son-in-law—and in some cases, the future parent of your grandchildren—you will begin to think more deeply about him or her. Are you thinking about his high school transcript? Or concerning yourself with the classes she took in college? Probably not. You are likely wanting to know what kind of person he or she is and whether or not he or she will be a good spouse to your child and a good parent to your future grandchildren.

Helping our students achieve in school and learn rigorous and relevant material is critical to helping them continue to advance successfully through the academic process. But as their lives progress through adulthood, it is often their character and their ability to engage respectfully and effectively with others that will make or break their continued, post-academic success—in careers and in personal relationships.

While the development of a child's character is first and foremost the responsibility of the family, schools can and should play a secondary and reinforcing role. Through our client work and interaction with schools at the International Center, we have determined twelve guiding principles of character that communities and employers believe must be cultivated in children in order for them to mature into high-functioning, productive adults. We have found that even the most divergent groups support these guiding principles.

The guiding principles are attributes of character that influence an individual's thoughts, feelings, and behavior. They direct personal and interpersonal behavior in any environment and in any situation, and they evolve over a lifespan—but only if they are instilled in the first place.

Schools can devise their own list of interpersonal skills necessary for a successful life or use the following twelve guiding principles:

1. **Adaptability:** The ability and willingness to change; putting oneself in harmony with changed circumstances

2. **Compassion:** Kindness; the desire to help others in need or distress

3. **Contemplation:** Giving serious consideration to something; thinking through things carefully

4. **Courage:** Bravery; the willingness to put beliefs into practice; the capacity to meet danger without giving way to fear

5. **Honesty:** Truthfulness, sincerity; never deceiving, stealing, or taking advantage of the trust extended by others

6. **Initiative:** Eagerness to do something; thinking and acting on one's own ideas without prompting by others

7. **Loyalty:** Faithfulness, dependability; being faithful to another person in the performance or duty or adhering to a contract with another person

8. **Optimism:** Positive beliefs; taking a hopeful view and believing that all will work out for the best

9. **Perseverance:** Working hard at something; trying hard and continuously in spite of obstacles and difficulties

10. **Respect:** Regard, value, admiration, appreciation; special esteem or consideration in which one holds another person or thing

11. **Responsibility:** Accountability; considering oneself answerable for something

12. **Trustworthiness:** Reliability, dependability; acting in a way that deserves trust and confidence from others

A note on the digital tattoo and how it relates to personal skill development. Most colleges and most large companies now staff a person dedicated to vetting candidates' online personas. The uncomfortable and unfortunate truth is that what our students put online today could stand in the way of their dream college or career tomorrow. Thanks to the permanence of social media, gone are the days where children can make youthfully naïve mistakes and learn from them. The digital tattoo adds a degree of urgency to teaching students the underpinnings of character in an effort to provide them the tools to make smart online choices. The digital tattoo can haunt students for decades and impede their college and career success. Therefore, I am of the belief that this demands greater onus be put on teachers to teach digital literacy. After all, it is our number one job to prepare students for successful futures.

Furthermore, because virtual interactions make hurtful behavior all too easy and common, we must remind students that the in-person behaviors we hold in such high regard are just as important and relevant online. Because their futures depend on it, we must teach our students that it's no longer enough to be a person of good character in real life, we have to be one online, too.

References

Berger, Ron (2013). Leaders of their own learning: Transforming schools through student-engaged assessment. New York: Wiley.

Bidwell, Allie (2013). "Millions of graduates hold jobs that don't require a college degree, report says." *The Chronicle of Higher Education*: http://chronicle.com/article/Millions-of-Graduates-Hold/136879/, 28 January 2013. Retrieved 17 February 2015.

Ellis, Blake (2013). "Class of 2013 grads average $35,200 in total debt." CNNMoney.com: http://money.cnn.com/2013/05/17/pf/college/student-debt/index.html, 17 May 2013. Retrieved 17 February 2015.

Greenstone, Michael and Adam Looney (2011). "Trends: Reduced earnings for men in America." Brookings Institute (2011): http://www.brookings.edu/research/papers/2011/07/men-earnings-greenstone-looney. Retrieved 12 January 2015.

Hattie, John (2009). *Visible learning: A synthesis of over 800 meta-analyses relating to achievement.* London: Routledge.

ManpowerGroup (2014). The talent shortage continues: How the ever changing role of HR can bridge the gap. Retrieved from www.ManpowerGroup.com.

Project Tomorrow (2013). From chalkboards to tablets: The emergence of the K-12 digital learner. Retrieved from www.tomorrow.org.

Sheninger, Eric (2014). *Digital leadership: Changing paradigms for changing times.* Thousand Oaks, Calif.: Corwin.

U.S. Department of Education (2014). New college graduates at work: Employment among 1992–93, 1999–2000, and 2007–08 Bachelor's Degree recipients 1 year after graduation. Retrieved from www.nces.ed.gov.

Part Two

The Daggett System
for Effective Instruction:
A Framework for Taking Control

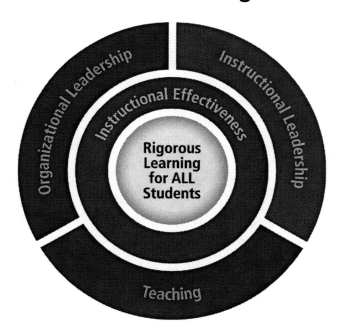

Chapter Four

It Takes Everyone

On September 16, 1985, my family's world changed forever. That was the day our son, Paul, 11 years old at the time, was hit by a car in front of our house. We almost lost him that afternoon. The accident scene was horrendous.

Rescue workers rushed Paul to the hospital, where he underwent several hours of surgery. All Bonnie and I could do was sit in the waiting room. Every hour or so, one of the doctors came out to give us an update. We were overcome with fear every time they did. Is he dead? Is he going to pull through? What would his life be like?

Over the years I've often thought about that day, and also this question: Who were the most important people at that hospital on that September day? The CEO? The president? The chairman of the board? Of course not. The most important people were the doctors treating Paul. I came to realize the entire hospital system, from the CEO to the accounting and janitorial departments, was *aligned* to let those doctors do what they do best. Every hospital's mission is to save lives—and the best ones do it by making sure they hire the best doctors, provide them with the best training and equipment, and then step aside and let them go to work.

Today, whenever I walk into one of this country's most rapidly improving schools, I am reminded of that hospital. In these top schools, teachers are the most important people in the system—not the superintendent, not the principals or assistant principals, not the school board. In these schools, the job of the principal is to clear the way for teachers so they can teach. It takes everyone, working as a team, working in alignment, to ensure that all students can learn.

Early in my career at the International Center, I learned that collecting and sharing a mix of best practices would not, in the long run, be enough to provide sustained, significant change for all students. We needed something more: a system. Over time, we developed what we call the Daggett System for Effective Instruction, or DSEI. This system focuses on three areas: (1) organizational leadership, to create a culture of high expectations and a shared vision; (2) instructional leadership, to provide the tools, training, data, and other assistance to develop teaching and instructional effectiveness; and (3) teaching, so teachers can meet the challenges of teaching in the twenty-first century.

We believe it takes a system, not just a teacher, to ensure student success. Here are some fervent examples of taking a systemwide approach.

The Story of Brockton High School

The city of Brockton will never be mistaken for Boston, its neighbor 24 miles to the north.

For decades, the "City of Champions" has been down on its luck. Crime, poverty, and homelessness are chronic. The city is best known as the home of heavyweight champion Rocky Marciano and also for manufacturing shoes—during the Civil War, Brockton was the shoe capital of the world. But the industry gradually moved overseas, and by the 1970s and 1980s, Brockton was without an economic foundation.

Yet the city remains stubbornly proud.

"There's something about this city," says Dr. Susan Szachowicz, a Brockton native and retired principal of Brockton High School. "There's this chip-on-your-shoulder pride. The Rocky mentality is not a joke. Even when you're punched and knocked down, our answer is, 'OK, we'll show you!' We used to play up that sentiment with our school kids. We'd tell them, 'People out there don't think you can make it, but we know you can.'"

Brockton High, with about 4,300 students, is the largest high school in the state. About two-thirds of the students qualify for free or reduced-price lunches. More than two-thirds are African-American or Latino. At least 14 percent are learning to speak English. Despite Brockton's challenges, there is something special about the place. Szachowicz describes it as a sense of community among staff and students that has endured for generations.

But academics? That was something else altogether. "Things were bad, really bad," Szachowicz says. "There were no standards. Teachers were almost like independent contractors; they could teach just about whatever they wanted."

In 1993, the state established the Massachusetts Comprehensive Assessment System, called MCAS for short. Under this system, students had to pass the MCAS test in order to graduate from high school. In 1998, the first set of MCAS scores showed 44 percent of tenth graders at Brockton failed English and 75 percent failed math.

The Search for Answers

Szachowicz, then the Department Head of Social Science, and a colleague were asked to create a leadership team to brainstorm how to turn things around. They recruited twenty teachers and staff members and named them to a group they called the Restructuring Committee. Their first order of business was to establish a mission and ground rules. The committee developed an ambitious, twofold mission: improve all students' achievement and personalize the education experience for every student. Establishing ground rules was fairly simple. First, members agreed that a respectful dialogue was essential. Second, a criticism of someone's suggestion had to be accompanied by another suggestion. Third, the committee agreed that discretion would be paramount. The group created a meeting schedule and went to work. (Szachowicz, 2013)

How do you bring about significant change? Members started asking questions: What do students need to know to be successful, not only in school, but also in their lives after school? How do we improve academic achievement and personalize the educational experience for all students? After several false starts, the committee settled on a radical concept: *literacy*. Every teacher, from the art teacher to the gym teacher, would be part of the plan. Everyone would teach literacy.

"That was the foundation," Szachowicz says. "We asked ourselves, 'What do we think our students will need beyond their lives at Brockton High?'" And the answer was reading, writing, speaking, and reasoning. In other words, literacy.

The committee introduced specific instructional strategies, such as a ten-step writing process that every student would follow. Members maintained an unwavering focus on implementing the process in every classroom, with no exceptions. Writing was incorporated into every subject, and teachers worked together to develop writing strategies.

Szachowicz and the committee believed nothing could be left to chance. They monitored students, faculty, and administration. They assessed students' mastery. They made sure faculty members taught literacy with fidelity. They made sure administrators assisted faculty, provided instructional feedback, and reviewed student work for consistency.

Today, literacy charts outlining the four literacy skills—reading, writing, speaking, and reasoning—hang in every classroom. "We changed the culture," Szachowicz says. "That's the best part of the Brockton High story. It tells a story that so rarely exists in schools."

In Her Own Words: Dr. Susan Szachowicz

Szachowicz was a student, teacher, and principal at Brockton High School in Brockton, Mass. She is now a senior fellow at the International Center for Leadership in Education. What follows is a question-and-answer session with her about transforming schools.

In transforming Brockton, you say you learned that you cannot teach to the test. Yet your superintendent told you to "just get those kids to pass." Isn't that teaching to the test?

If not for the MCAS, Brockton would not have tried to change. That test was a hammer. But while the test was the initial motivator, we learned it couldn't be our primary and whole focus. One of the big mistakes we made at first was focusing on the test. We were trying to out-guess the test, and you just can't. Having said that, in the end you do need to take care of the test—and I think every school does. You are judged externally by it, so you have to take care of it. But the test is just a baseline. The question becomes, what do our students need to succeed on the MCAS, and then more importantly, what do they need to succeed in class *and* in their lives beyond school.

How did you arrive at literacy as the solution?

The Restructuring Committee was a real think tank. We went back and looked at the test, but instead of looking at the content, we looked at the skills our students would need to pass it. We noticed that we did poorly in writing. It really leapt out at us. The MCAS required a lot of writing, and our kids were leaving those questions blank or barely writing anything. It was clear they weren't prepared for writing. That was the genesis of the literacy initiative.

Was it difficult working with teachers' unions?

Sure we had issues, but you have to figure out what you can control and what you can't. Brockton has a very strong teachers' union and we had some big battles, but there were certain things I had no control over so I didn't fuss about them. We worked within the parameters of the contract. For the literacy initiative, we trained all the teachers and made sure all the union leadership understood the plan, so when it came time to implement, everyone was on board.

What's your role at the International Center?

I'm working in two areas: literacy and leadership. I'm really interested in leadership because you can have the best program in the world, but if it's put into the hands of an underperforming teacher or ineffective leader, it won't go anywhere. The leadership element is huge.

Where do you see K–12 education in 10 years?

I know one thing: K–12 educators can't pull the covers over our heads anymore. In this day and age, you've got competition from charters, private schools, home-schooling, and virtual schools. Parents can vote with their feet if they are not happy. With technology, it's hard to know what future schools will look like. But I know schools will still be important because relationships are so important. Relationships are huge. Thinking and reasoning will also be important. I think schools will have a powerful place in society, but the classrooms might look very different.

How is Brockton High doing today?

I think the best part of the Brockton story is now. What happens in most cases is that when a leader leaves, things crumble and go back to the old ways. But we changed the culture at Brockton. It's now all about sustained, consistent improvement. Brockton High is better than ever.

The Story of Raise Your Hand Texas

Raise Your Hand Texas (RYHT) is a nonprofit organization whose mission is to improve public schools in Texas by developing strong building principals and by involving itself in public policy. Charles C. Butt, chairman of the H-E-B supermarket chain—with more than 300 stores and $17 billion in sales—started RYHT in 2006 as a way to promote higher student achievement.

One of the ways RYHT accomplishes this is by providing high-quality professional development to principals and aspiring principals. RYHT partners with us at the International Center and also with Harvard and Rice University to provide coaching and other support. To date, more than 800 principals have attended Harvard through the Raise Your Hand Texas Leadership Program. They spend a week at Harvard in the summer absorbing the latest best practices and then return ready to empower teachers to succeed.

The program at Rice is called the Rice Education Entrepreneurship program, which is taught through the university's Jones Graduate School of Business. It is a 12-month program where principals study to earn a business certificate. They attend classes Thursday evening, all day Friday, and all day Saturday 9–10 times a year, and then attend an intensive 10-week session in the summer.

Strong student achievement depends on strong principals. A study by three professors about the impact of principals found that an effective principal raises achievement by between two and seven months of learning in a single school year. (Branch, Hanushek, and Rivkin, 2012) But the increasing demands on principals are staggering. More mandates, decentralized decision-making, and sophisticated technology make the job more difficult than ever. "A high-quality principal can take a mid-level teacher and make him or her into a strong teacher," says Dr. David Anthony, CEO of RYHT, who was a principal for nine years and a superintendent for 24 years. "You have to have that person clearing the obstacles, providing the structure, the discipline, and the resources for teachers. That's how they get better."

To RYHT, public education is an investment, not a cost. The organization is heavily involved in statewide education policy. "Our mindset is to discover and identify the policies that need to change in order to improve education," Anthony says. "We're not just in there trying to make political decisions. We use data and research so we can be research-based, data-driven, and experienced-based as well. That's what separates us from the people who are just out there writing policy for political platforms. Our approach is based on what is best for the educational environment for students in Texas. It's a holistic approach to transform education."

In His Own Words: Dr. David Anthony

Anthony's educational career has spanned 40 years as a teacher, principal, and superintendent. He joined Raise Your Hand Texas as CEO in 2011. What follows is a question-and-answer session with him about transforming schools.

Tell us a little bit about the name of your group.

Raise Your Hand Texas means taking a stand, making a pledge to support public education by getting involved in your local school. You can't have good schools unless you work at a local level. You have to have people step in and get involved: you can't do it just from the top down. Have we ever considered changing our name? Several times, but in the end we are very well known in Texas. Plus, it's certainly a conversation piece when you put the name on your business card and then try to explain it.

How has your background as a principal and superintendent helped you at RYHT?

I was a principal for nine years, a superintendent for 24 years, and a classroom teacher for four years. I was 25 years old when I became principal of one of the worst schools in Louisiana. At 25, you're idealistic and high-energy—you want to change the world, and in this case, I really had to. I learned how to be a good principal from great teachers, not by getting my certification or by taking classes in college. I spent my first six months as principal in master teachers' classrooms, and those teachers taught me what they did and what they needed to succeed in the classroom. I've never forgotten that. Within three years, we took that failing school and made it into one of the best. Those teachers taught me well. Looking back, that was one of my most rewarding times in public education.

What role, if any, should central administration play in improving student performance?

You have no sustainability without the central office. Superintendents come and go, but the central office staff generally doesn't. So if they are not on the same page with you, and if they are not well trained, and if they are not in sync with the principals, you'll have serious infighting. Everything depends on having a central office that is part of your team. If you have a central office that is well-trained and committed, then you will absolutely sustain any improvements you have made. It's critical.

What makes a good superintendent?

A big heart. A thick skin. And a willingness to make decisions every day that support students. I've always told myself that the day I make a decision that helps me keep my job rather than doing what's best for the kids, that's the day I need to be fired. You have to accept all the blame and give away all the credit. You have to develop your people and hire people who are smarter and better than you are. You have to enjoy conflict. If you can't aggressively argue, then you will never know how people truly feel. And once you know how they feel, you may find out that their idea is the best one. You have to create an environment based on respect and relationships. If you don't know your custodian's name, who the best bus driver is, or who the best food service person is, and if you don't make them part of the team, you're never going to have a cohesive district. Building and nurturing all the relationships is a full-time job. [University of Alabama football coach] Bear Bryant used to say, "If we win, the kids did a great job, but if we lose, I did a lousy job of coaching." That's pretty much the way I look at things.

What was a major success for RYHT in the last year or so?

I think the most important thing we've accomplished is our coaching program run through the International Center. We've found that strong coaching is the most important thing we can do for principals at any level. A coach goes in and works with a principal at least one day every month and follows up with emails and phone calls. The coaches give the principals assignments and ask them to develop a principal improvement plan that is tied to a campus improvement plan. This helps the principals understand that if their campuses are not doing well, then neither are they. It shows them their weaknesses and what they need to focus on. The coach does not hire or fire the principal. The coach does not evaluate the principal, and because of that, the coach and principal develop a tight bond. It's amazingly effective.

Any final thoughts?

I love what Bill Daggett says about public education: every district, every campus has its own DNA. There is no one-size-fits-all cure. You have to find out what makes a district or a building tick, and then go in there and try to change it for the better. Everyone's looking for the silver bullet or the magic potion, but there's no such thing. Bill is one of the few people—maybe the only person—I've ever dealt with who gets that.

References

Branch, Gregory F., Eric A. Hanushek, and Steven G. Rivkin (2012). "Estimating the effect of leaders on public sector productivity: The case of school principals" (Working Paper No. 17803). http://www.nber.org/papers/w17803. Retrieved from the National Bureau of Economic Research website.

Szachowicz, Susan (2013). *Transforming Brockton High School: High standards, high expectations, no excuses.* Rexford, N.Y.: International Center for Leadership in Education.

Chapter Five

How Do We Get Started?

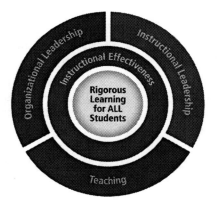

What is your vision for students? What are your core values as a teacher, as a school? What are your goals? How will you achieve them? What is the service you want to provide for students, and who do you want them to become upon graduation? What do you believe about student learning and achievement?

Most schools haven't done this deep soul searching—but if you want to change your school, it's where you must begin. You must also be prepared to take on the change, to be the change. Remember, most people say they want change—as long as it doesn't affect them.

High-performing schools have an absolutely crystal clear vision of what they want to accomplish. They also have a culture that supports and encourages positive change. *Culture trumps strategy.* Until you can articulate a vision, you will just be spinning your wheels. Until you have a positive culture, any strategy you employ will fail, guaranteed.

At the International Center, we've spent 24 years identifying and understanding how our country's best schools do what they do. Taking what we've learned, we developed the Daggett System for Effective Instruction, or DSEI. But it all starts with a vision.

It Takes a System, Not Just a Teacher

Research supports what most of us see as common sense: the relationship between a teacher and a student is essential to high-level learning. But effective teaching is not the end goal; it is merely a way to get to the ultimate goal—student achievement. At the International Center, rigorous learning for ALL students is our core belief. We believe all kids can learn. And *all* means *ALL*.

With that said, can all kids learn the same things at the same time and in the same way? My wife and I have five adult children. They are dramatically different in their interests, personalities, and aptitudes. Academically, they ran the gamut from a gifted and talented student, to a pretty good student, to an average student, to two students with disabilities, one of whom is Audrey. Audrey has an intellectual disability, autism, and epilepsy. Anyone who thinks she can achieve academically what her four older siblings did is more than naïve. But she can—and does—learn. In many ways, the academic, social, and personal gains she made in school are actually greater than those of her older siblings.

And, as I mentioned, our son Paul was hit by a car when he was 11. He was in a coma and on life support for several months. He all but lost the ability to speak and hear. He had such severe ataxia that he couldn't write. But he's a four-year college graduate from Marist College in Poughkeepsie, N.Y. Paul doesn't have a good job—he's got a great job. The academic, social, and personal gains Paul experienced in our schools is even greater than that of our first children. The larger point here is this: based on my own personal experience, both as a father and as a teacher, I know that ALL kids can learn given the proper conditions. But I don't believe they can all achieve the same thing. That's one of my core beliefs.

How do we develop the proper conditions so that ALL students can become all they are capable of being? You need to build a system. It takes a total system to develop, maintain, and enhance effective instruction. Put another way, central administration and building principals must align themselves to support teachers. Because we believe teachers have the most influence on instruction, the entire system must work to make teachers effective. We need top-down support for bottom-up success.

DSEI was born from the research-derived realization that, despite the fact that teachers have the most critical and direct impact on students, they cannot, in isolation, effect true change. It takes strong organizational leadership to galvanize the entire school around a vision of high expectations for students *and* staff. And it takes strong instructional leadership to ensure that teachers have what they need to improve student achievement. It is these three areas—organizational leadership, instructional leadership, and teaching—that are the focus of DSEI.

We Need Leaders at Every Level

Before we get into the nuts and bolts of DSEI, it's important to have a conversation about leadership.

Who are your leaders? Many of you might point to the superintendent, or perhaps various building principals, or even a few outstanding teachers. You might be right, but there's another way to look at the issue—one we've found to be far more powerful. Leadership is a function, not just a person. It is a disposition, not a position. Leadership is about a mentality, a structure, a focus, a passion, and a commitment to creating an environment where students thrive.

All too often I see people look to an organizational chart to determine the leadership team. When this happens, everyone outside of the top bracket of the chart sees his or her ability to drive change diminished; potential is squandered, opportunities are lost. If we want to reorient the entire educational system to one that puts students first, then we must rethink leadership, and in a way that is inclusive of everyone.

Leadership can—and must—come from all levels in the educational system. A central administrator can recommend and oversee implementation of a new data analytics tool to measure long-term student improvement. The PE teacher can be a leader in driving an interdisciplinary approach to physical education. (Football, after all, is about applied math and science.) The cafeteria head could take a leadership role in spearheading a "real jobs" initiative where students can apply for jobs, like helping manage inventory in the cafeteria, to gain hands-on job skills. A chemistry teacher could build a team of teachers to implement a curriculum-wide writing practice to improve literacy. The librarian could seek and find a partner from a local media company to lead a workshop on vetting online sources.

Great leaders will inspire leadership in everyone. With great leadership comes great responsibility. But it's time to rise to the occasion and put our students' interests in front of our own. Twenty-first century learning requires a twenty-first century take on leadership, one where leadership is encouraged, cultivated, and available to anyone with the desire to put student-centered initiatives into motion.

Organizational Leadership

It is up to organizational leadership to create a districtwide culture where leadership is regarded as a disposition, not a position, a force inhabitable by anyone with the will.

Once you've created a broad awareness that modern leadership is a mindset, the desire to turn ideas into action, then what? How do you tap this enormous potential sitting within every person in the entire system to drive rapid improvement?

As part of DSEI, we've identified six steps that organizational leadership must take to arrive at that ideal point where everyone feels comfortable asserting his or her leadership in the name of putting students first.

But first, a note on how organizational leadership and instructional leadership must collaborate in this endeavor for positive change. If a school wants to see rapid improvement, school leaders would be wise to adopt the overarching elements of organizational leadership. What we at the International Center have come to learn through recent research and work with districts is that if a school wants *sustained* improvement, it must have alignment with and support from the central office. District office leadership must work in tandem with leadership at each of its schools. When this district–school partnership in a shared vision happens, then the entire *district* will rapidly improve.

The six primary elements of organizational leadership follow:

1. **Create a culture of high academic expectations and positive relationships.** *Culture trumps strategy.* If you take away nothing else from this book, please remember that one sentence. Culture dictates how a team faces challenges. Without a positive culture, you've got nothing. Without a positive culture, you can't begin to deal with a generation of wired, tech-savvy students who are growing up in a digital world and finding their analog schools less and less relevant. Without a positive culture, you can't come to grips with an increasingly technological and global economy where graduating students must innovate and compete more than ever just to stay afloat. And frankly and perhaps most importantly, without a positive culture, you lack the environment to rally and unify everyone around your vision and goals; morale and inspiration are byproducts of a strong culture.

2. **Establish a shared vision and communicate it to all constituent groups.** Let's ask those questions we asked at the start of the chapter again. What's your vision? What are your core beliefs? Once you do the hard work to establish a vision, you will to need to align all goals and action plans to it, and in a way that all stakeholders can understand, contribute to, and commit to.

3. **Align organizational structures and systems to the vision.** Once you've developed the culture and articulated the vision, the next step is to organize a system that supports the newly established vision and goals. That there is a system in place to direct all decisions must be broadly and clearly communicated. It must become a districtwide habit that when building any new program, initiative, team, or department, everyone should always ask, "Does this advance and support our vision?" Organizational leadership must also align the vision and

structures to ensure literacy, math, and technology integration across all grade levels and disciplines.

4. **Build leadership capacity through an empowerment model.** Organizational leadership must be able to identify and cultivate emerging future leaders. It must also aid in building leadership teams where the aim is to diversify skill sets and empower strengths on the path to raising student achievement. This kind of distributed leadership not only makes teachers feel broadly supported, it also paves the way for continuous development and growth of new leaders who, in turn, can help transform a district or school, and, eventually, maintain and evolve a vision.

5. **Align teacher/leader selection, support, and evaluation.** Many schools today have become consumed by the new teacher evaluation requirements and have lost sight of the fact that they should be focusing on selection, support, and evaluation on an ongoing continuum. They are losing control instead of taking control. In turn, teachers are growing increasingly demoralized and burnt out. To regain control, organizational leaders need to look beyond just mandated evaluations and focus on a total "talent management" system, where recruitment, retention, development, and evaluation are aligned to vision and goals. The key is to provide an approach that lets teachers and leaders reach their personal and professional goals as they simultaneously support student achievement.

6. **Support decision-making with relevant data systems.** Data systems and effective data analysis are essential to monitoring student improvement and progress. They also provide key insights to make learning rigorous and relevant for all students. Organizational leaders must employ appropriate data systems and provide any necessary training at all levels.

Instructional Leadership

Instructional leadership is directly and ultimately focused on rigorous learning for ALL students, though it is only through teacher support and training that this is accomplished. The ultimate aim of instructional leadership is to empower teachers to apply strategies and best practices that put students at the center of active learning. The DSEI framework outlines the following six instructional leadership elements to support teachers:

1. **Use research to establish the urgent need to promote higher academic expectations and positive relationships.** The first job of instructional leadership is to reinforce the vision set forth by the organizational leadership. To do this, instructional leadership needs to clearly communicate to all constituents the process that will be used to achieve academic, social, and emotional excellence. One of the most effective ways to do this is to use research and authoritative testimony that corroborates the urgent need to raise the bar in student achievement and the instruction that must be delivered to get students there. Instructional leaders must also see themselves as "change agents" in raising standards and expectations.

2. **Develop, implement, and monitor standards-aligned curriculum and assessments.** Instructional leaders have an admittedly tricky task. They must develop, implement, and monitor a curriculum and assessment process that matches the school vision. But they must also incorporate any required state standards. Thus, instructional leaders are charged with the task of integrating vision-driven processes with state standards, and doing so in a way that can be clearly articulated and easily monitored so that teachers have a tangible grasp on how they are being evaluated. I have found that an interdisciplinary approach to learning is the most effective strategy for finding alignment between vision and mandated standards, while also increasing rigor and relevance. By focusing on an interdisciplinary curriculum, leaders remain in control of how standards fit into their teaching strategy rather than allowing outside forces to direct strategy.

3. **Integrate literacy, math, and technology across all disciplines.** This is critical. Today's high-paying careers demand high level, integrative, reason-based thinking and an ability to navigate technology. All teachers at all grades and across all subjects

must assume responsibility for delivering an education that arms students with the skills that will be required of them in college and careers. New standards underscore the heightened emphasis on broad-based literacy development, with a focus on text complexity and practical applications of literacy. They also focus on the "standards of mathematical practice," which include such skills as adaptive reasoning, strategic competence, conceptual understanding, procedural fluency, and productive disposition. Use of technology should be incorporated wherever and whenever possible to better reflect the working world students will face.

4. **Facilitate data-driven decision-making to inform instruction**. As I mentioned in Chapter Three, that there are so many new data analytics tools out there to facilitate data collection is a boon to schools, as data can provide powerful insights into each student's—and teacher's—strengths and weaknesses. To make learning rigorous and relevant to all students, instructional leaders must make use of data analytics tools, provide training around them, and work with teachers to understand the data and turn it into actionable instruction and interventions.

5. **Provide opportunities for professional learning, collaboration, and growth focused on high-quality instruction and increased student learning**. Standards require that sustained and high-quality professional development takes place, but all too often it looks haphazard and cursory—a mere attempt to check a box. Our teachers deserve better, and so do our students. Instructional leaders must use the most relevant data and research to determine the professional learning needs of their teaching staff. Importantly, learning must maximize teacher growth but also have a direct improvement impact on student learning. Clearly articulated assessments must be put in place that measure any professional development initiative in terms of its impact on both the teacher *and* the student.

6. **Engage family and community in the learning process**. Several studies show that when family members and the community are engaged in schools, student achievement goes up. Generally,

this happens across the board, and therefore, the achievement gap can begin to close. The challenge is figuring out how to get families involved when more and more parents have to work full-time to make ends meet or have language barriers that might preclude comfort in school involvement. Innovative schools are finding creative ways for parents to engage flexibly in their children's learning. They are also developing initiatives to forge stronger ties to the community to reinforce for students a feeling of consistent support from several arenas, while also showing students the importance of a positive contribution to the local community.

Teaching

Let's make this crystal clear: in today's most rapidly improving schools, teachers are the most important people in the system. Not the superintendent. Not the principal. In fact, the job of the superintendent and the principal is to clear the way for teachers to do what they need to do to promote rigorous learning.

If organizational leadership does its job of establishing an overarching vision and mission, and if instructional leaders make sure teachers receive all forms of support, then teachers will be well supported in addressing the daunting challenges of today's classroom.

DSEI includes six elements to ensure successful teaching for the twenty-first century:

1. **Build effective instruction based on *rigorous and relevant* expectations.** We have seen it time and time again: teachers who believe ALL students can achieve to their potential are far more effective and successful. So too are their students. When students feel respected and cared for, they are inherently motivated and they expand their capacity for rigorous learning.

2. **Create and implement an effective learner environment that is engaging and aligned to learner needs.** Teachers must create a learning environment that addresses students' personal, social, and emotional needs. They must strive to engage all learners and know each student on an individual level. A strong, caring

relationship between students and teachers has repeatedly been proven to enhance a student's commitment to his or her own learning.

3. **Possess and continue to develop content area knowledge and make it relevant to the learner.** While subject area expertise is important, effective teaching today is more than just a transmittal of knowledge. It's about the ability to make connections, show relevance, nurture engagement, and enhance understanding through application to real-world scenarios that resonate with students. As we know, relevance makes rigor possible. With systemic support, teachers need to stay informed on the most current pedagogy and content to amplify their ability to contextualize subject knowledge within the outside world.

4. **Plan and provide learning experiences using effective research-based strategies that are embedded with best practices, including the use of technology.** Plenty of recent cognitive research shows that technology is changing how we process information. Imagine, then, how much it has changed the brains of the generation raised on technology! We educators must understand and accept that how today's students learn and absorb information is just different from how we did when the world was primarily analog.

All teachers need a versatile and comprehensive repertoire of instructional strategies so they can match teaching approaches to both learning objectives and the individual learning styles of students. But all of these strategies must fit with how today's generation learns. To achieve this, teachers must keep on top of the latest research about how our students process and filter information. In short, we have to teach today's students—not yesterday's.

To raise the level of rigor and relevance, we have found enormous value in adding in culturally relevant learning where possible. It's also an easy way to involve families, which is proven not only to increase student achievement, but also to begin to close the student achievement gap. The more that families can actively engage in their children's learning, the better.

5. **Use assessments and data to guide and differentiate instruction**. Formative assessments are informal and occur frequently in real-time, and summative assessments provide more long-term, comprehensive data after the fact. Both provide data that can help teachers grasp a student's progress and determine how to differentiate instruction based on where and why a student is having difficulty. The most effective teachers develop a habit of regularly asking themselves, "Did each student get it? How do I know they got it? How do I help those students who didn't?" The goal of asking such questions is to be proactive, not reactive, by helping teachers spot a student's misunderstanding before it spins out of control.

6. **Further content and instructional knowledge through continuous professional learning that is both enriching and collaborative**. We are asking teachers today to do things they were never trained to do. There must be an incredible commitment to professional development—and not just traditional workshops or unfocused staff development days. Teachers will need time and a safe environment to practice and develop today's skills of effective instruction. Only through a system that supports teacher development, collaboration, and professional practices will teachers be able to create learning environments that result in improved student achievement.

So that's DSEI in a nutshell. We will delve deeper into each segment in the ensuing chapters.

My aim in this book is to soften DSEI, to distill its most critical and salient points, to drill down to its heart and soul. And that is that DSEI is a high-level framework for rigorous and relevant learning and student achievement—from the classroom all the way to the boardroom. It's also a tool to take control of our districts, our schools, and our classrooms amid the fog of external demands. It's a systemwide approach to education delivery that makes sure the needs of students trump any and all other needs or motives, while still keeping an eye on teachers' professional goals and development. DSEI is a way to think about what we believe about children, schools, and learning in the currently complex, confusing, and convoluted context of American education, where standards, assessments, accountability, and teacher evaluation systems are colliding with budgets, the global economy, technological innovation, wired kids, and public policy debates.

DSEI recognizes the primacy and immeasurable value of great teachers and great teaching and strives to align systems so that teachers get what they need to provide the best support for today's learners.

After all, rigorous learning is the ultimate goal.

After we take a closer look at each DSEI segment and its elements in the ensuing chapters, you'll reach the Best Practices reference section, where we've provided a best practice for each element. After all, all these goals and great intentions around student-centered learning must be realized.

As I mentioned in the Introduction, eventually this book had to go to print. We remain committed to growing and evolving our collection of field-tested best practices. Please check back with us at the International Center for our newest best practices.

Chapter 6

A Closer Look: Organizational Leadership

Almost by definition, if you work in central administration you are far removed from the classroom and that all-important student-teacher relationship. Historically we've understood that the relationship between student and teacher is crucial. More recently, educators have focused on the concept of "principal as instructional leader" to strengthen the student-teacher bond. But central administration? What is its role?

My colleagues and I have the privilege of working with school districts of all sizes and organizational configurations. We are working with districts that are so small that the superintendent is the only administrator in the district. We are also working with several of the nation's largest districts, where the central administration has several hundred employees with more than 20 assistant and deputy superintendents. The majority of districts fall somewhere between these ends of the spectrum.

But no matter its size, central administration is a bureaucracy struggling with board and community relations, finances, operations, and curriculum. Unfortunately, it's not uncommon to see average and even poor-performing employees sprinkled throughout central administration.

The relationship between central administration and student achievement has, until recently, typically not been as direct and defined as it needs to be. But that point of view is starting to shift. We're beginning to understand that central administration plays a critical and necessary role in our best performing districts.

Through the financial support of Raise Your Hand Texas, we have been working with numerous districts across the state. Using the same set of consultants with the same tools, strategies, and support, we experienced great success in some schools and little success in others. We were puzzled. What was the common denominator—if any—at these chronically underperforming schools? RYHT enlisted the Data Wise Project to help. Based at the Harvard Graduate School of Education, Data Wise helps educators analyze the reams of data districts typically produce. After analyzing the numbers, Data Wise concluded there was indeed a common denominator: lack of adequate leadership from central administration. It was an aha moment for all of us.

As I said in the prior chapter, schools themselves can—and must—build a strong vision and culture. They too can incorporate the principles of organizational leadership on a smaller scale. But if schools hope to see newfound improvements hold up over the long term, particularly as school staff come and go, their district office must have strong organizational leadership working in tandem with schools toward a shared vision and aligned goals. Dr. David Anthony, CEO of Raise Your Hand Texas, said it best in Chapter Four: "Everything depends on having a central office that is part of your [school's] team. If you have a central office that is well trained and committed, then you will absolutely sustain any improvements you have made. It's critical."

Element 1: Culture, Culture, Culture

How should central administration exert its leadership? Here's a hint: *Culture trumps strategy.* Yes, central administration must develop a culture of high expectations across the district, a culture that reflects the twenty-first century world we live in, where the needs of students trump the self-serving interests of adults. That's the only way to sustain meaningful change.

Creating a culture of high expectations is mission critical. But the hard truth is that it's incredibly difficult to achieve. One main reason is that most people resist change, even if they say they support it—no change for me, thank you. Somehow, some way, central administration must create awareness that there's a problem. And then slowly, central administrators must nurture a districtwide change in mentality.

Why the need for a mentality change? I've already mentioned that public education is improving, that schools have raised their standards and found ways to measure how well students are achieving them. Today more than ever, we're able to identify failing schools and provide effective improvement efforts. So yes, schools are changing for the better. The problem is they're not changing fast enough.

Let's look back for a moment:

- As of 2014, more than 70 percent of all 17–24-year-olds are not eligible to enlist in the military; that number is expected to climb to 80 percent within 10 years. Millions from this age group won't graduate from high school—and you can't enlist if you don't earn your diploma. A significant portion of those who do graduate won't pass a mandatory admissions test with a heavy emphasis on reading, writing, and math. Others will be disqualified by health issues.

  Recall, the business community went ballistic when they heard these statistics. *If young people are not qualified to join the military, what makes you think they can work for us?* Johnny or Susie may be able to get a job at the local convenience store or a fast food restaurant, but they don't have the skills to earn enough money to live on their own. If you play that out over time, you're left with the terrifying possibility that 70–80 percent of our young people are potentially headed for public assistance.

Still think we don't need a mentality change in our schools? Remember the chapter on the five emerging trends? Are schools anticipating these?

- Today's students are digital learners, but when they come to school, they power down their devices. Schools need to stop fighting the losing battle against technology and instead welcome technology and let it transform instruction. Schools will flourish if they embrace both digital learning and are willing to disrupt traditional teaching systems in the name of inventing a hybrid model, where teachers facilitate learning instead of just delivering instruction. Most schools are not doing this.
- The workplace and career landscape has fundamentally changed, and our education system has not kept pace. Technology is replacing workers, taking over mid-level, good-paying jobs. As the missing middle becomes more entrenched, job opportunities will sit overwhelmingly on the extreme ends of the spectrum—low-skilled or high-skilled. Well-paying careers require increasingly sophisticated skills. Workers must be taught fundamental technology skills so that from there, they have the ability to constantly learn new tasks in a technological, information-based environment. Today, many students simply are not career ready—because not enough of us are teaching them to be so.
- Students will not learn unless they believe school is relevant. Put another way, relevance makes rigor possible. But what's relevant to one student is not relevant to the next. In an earlier chapter, I used my grandchildren to make that point: I've got one who believes he's going to play football in the National Football League. I've got another who believes he's going to be a world-class musician. So how do you make school relevant to each one? One way is to teach math and science through football and use music and art to teach language arts. But you

need an organizational structure to do this. Today, most schools don't know how to organize themselves to support innovative methods to teach core subjects.

- Our education system focuses on tests to measure a student's degree of mastery at a given point in time, but it has not focused on the ongoing growth of a student over time. Only a few schools have changed their focus to a continuous improvement model for every student.

- Finally, this: today's schools are not doing enough to develop personal skills, nor are they teaching students that how we're expected to behave in the physical world is the same as how we need to behave in the digital world. Life today is much more than mastering math, science, language arts, and social studies. Personal and interpersonal skills like responsibility, self-motivation, integrity, honesty, collaboration, and leadership are critical in today's workplace. Most schools don't teach these softer skills, and most certainly don't teach it within the context of the Internet.

Convinced yet? We must change our mindsets. We must change our schools. And it's time we change our districts. We're out of excuses.

Element 2: Create a Vision

With so many challenges on our plate, we at the International Center believe that districts have no choice but to take on a greater role in creating a vision and encouraging their schools to do the same. In fact, we're calling on them to do so. Schools will only benefit from their district's support and influence in moving the system into the twenty-first century.

Once organizational leaders develop a culture that promotes change, then they work together to develop a vision from that culture. In creating a vision, we might ask, what does a twenty-first century learner need to know? What must he or she be able to do? Or, how does a school know if it is serving its students well and helping them become lifelong learners?

We asked these very questions when, in 2005, we began a five-year project to determine how we could turn 75 "promising" high schools across the country into proven models of success. Over the duration of the study—which was done in partnership with the Council of Chief State School Officers and the Successful Practices Network, with the support of the Bill & Melinda Gates Foundation—we found numerous examples of successful and rapidly improving schools. We identified common strands running through their cultures, shared visions, approaches to school improvement, and best practices. With the assistance of my colleague, Ray McNulty, we synthesized and summarized them into what we call the Learning Criteria. We've since found that the Learning Criteria is an excellent tool to help turn a school's culture into a shared vision of student achievement.

Defining the Learning Criteria
The Learning Criteria contains four components:

1. **Foundational learning,** which is learning core subjects like language arts, math, and science. It's also the information students will need to succeed on state tests. Foundational learning looks at a school's academic strengths. Mastering foundational learning is essential—but not adequate—in today's world. It's the minimum students must learn.
2. **Stretch learning,** which demonstrates rigorous and relevant learning beyond the minimum foundational requirements. When students are stretched, they are, for example, encouraged to participate in interdisciplinary activities and competitions, enroll in honors courses, pursue career majors, or satisfy requirements for specialized certificates.
3. **Personal skill development,** which in today's world has to extend from Pre-K through Grade 12 and college if we want our students to achieve success in their lives—professional and personal—beyond school. We have identified 12 personal attributes that schools need to cultivate in students for career readiness: *adaptability, loyalty, compassion, optimism, contemplation,*

perseverance, respect, courage, honesty, responsibility, initiative, and *trustworthiness.*

4. **Learner engagement**, which is the overarching dimension of the Learning Criteria, is both the prerequisite and the unifying theme for achieving success. Learner engagement means getting students motivated and committed to learning. The single most important lesson we have learned at the International Center is that *relevance makes rigor possible.* When we can captivate learners' attention, their performance improves dramatically—and, importantly, they feel a sense of satisfaction, belonging, and accomplishment. Consequently, they exhibit positive behaviors. Of course the challenge is that relevance is not a one-size-fits-all concept. It's personal. You must get to know each student and what makes him or her tick. Thus, relationships are key to learner engagement.

By thinking and talking through the components of the Learning Criteria and by vetting your system against its framework, a vision of what you want to be as a district, a school, a leader, and a teacher, and of what you want your students to gain under your care, will begin to emerge.

Let me illustrate the point another way. Some day, your son or daughter will come home with a significant other. When that happens, what's more important, that this newfound friend scored well on the state test, or that he or she possesses at least some of the personal skills that the Learning Criteria addresses? What do you hope for when new neighbors move in next door, that their college transcripts were strong, or that they are trustworthy and responsible? How many people have ever lost a job because of poor academics? Or was it because they lacked initiative and perseverance when the going got tough?

To the dismay of most educators, schools have become so fixated on test scores that we have unintentionally lost focus on these personal attributes. More importantly, we don't measure them—although we used to. Early in my career, our report cards would include a letter grade for each subject and also a short narrative about the student's overall performance and character:

Susan only averaged a C this semester, but she is a hard worker. She listens carefully to instructions and is polite. She is quite popular with her classmates and is developing into a leader; that's why her classmates elected her vice president. If Susan keeps plugging away, I know she can bring her average up to a B minus. She is a delight to have in class.

Today, comments like that have all but disappeared from most report cards—several schools stopped using them because we became totally focused on state tests. Which leads me to this question: *are we measuring what is easy to measure, or are we measuring what is most important?* One of the reasons many schools no longer measure a student's personal characteristics is that it's hard and subjective.

Unfortunately I believe that most schools start—and end—with teaching foundational learning. They never get past that point. But our model schools start by focusing on personal skill development and engaging all students. That's the tougher road, but if you start there, foundational learning and stretch learning will take care of themselves.

What kind of district, leader, school, or teacher do you want to be? Do you want to teach only to the foundational level? Or do you want to knock it out of the park and teach the student as a whole person to prepare him or her for the future? What's your vision?

If your central administration has created a culture, and you've developed a vision that focuses on foundational learning, stretch learning, developing personal skills, and engaging all students, the issue becomes this: Are you organizing your schools to accomplish this vision? How do you organize your staff to get there?

Element 3: Align Structures and Systems

Unfreeze. Transition. Refreeze. Those are the three stages of a well-known and widely used change management model from professor and psychologist Kurt Lewin. In the unfreezing stage of this model, a system prepares for change by understanding why and what needs to change. I like to think of it as "unfreezing" our structures and systems from the status of sacred and untouchable so that they can be objectively appraised against the newfound culture and vision.

Once vision is clear and leadership has begun to corral the support of the entire school, then all structures and systems must also be aligned to the ultimate goal. But the thing is, we have to be honest about why we're protecting some of the systems of the twentieth century. Is it because of someone's personal preference or belief? Is it easier or more convenient? Are we kowtowing to a vocal minority? Have we ever even paused to ask why we have this particular structure? Are we a school controlled by structures and systems, like the bell schedule, calendars, rooms teacher are used to teaching in, contract provisions, etc.? Are we simply protecting our own self-serving interests? Or are we a school dictated by vision?

When it comes to changing a school or district, function needs to dictate form. What a structure or system does to advance the vision should dictate its use; twenty-first century structures and systems need to emerge from a twenty-first century vision.

Through my work at the International Center, I have seen this time and time again—a school will attempt to implement a best practice that we've seen work with great success elsewhere. But it won't work in this particular school. Why? Because they've tried to square peg–round hole the practice into a system that wasn't aligned for innovative teaching.

If you want any hope of proven best practices and twenty-first century innovations having a positive effect on student achievement, they must be plugged into an entire system prepared for twenty-first century learning—which is the ultimate point of DSEI. It should also be noted that any twenty-first century learning structure should be built to integrate literacy, math, and technology across grade levels and disciplines.

Element 4: Build Leadership Capacity and Teams

At the start of Chapter Four, I told you about my son Paul's accident. Every single person involved in saving his life did what he or she needed to do to get Paul as urgently as possible, and in the best shape possible, to the care of the doctors. The police alerted the ambulance operator. The ENTs measured Paul's vitals as the driver expertly and quickly got him to the emergency room, where doctors had been alerted to be on standby. Then the doctors and nurses collaborated to save Paul's life.

Consider how many different systems and departments were involved in caring for Paul. There was leadership at every point, and all of that leadership was aligned to do one thing: get Paul under doctors' care so they could do what they do best. Paul lived because all efforts were mutually driven and supported by a diverse team of leaders, each operating toward the same objective.

In the nation's most rapidly improving schools, teachers feel as broadly and uniformly supported as the doctors were. But it takes distributed leadership to achieve an organization structure built upon letting teachers do what they do best: helping students achieve.

Systems and organizations work best when:

- Distributed leadership is aligned around a collaborative blend of skill sets, with each empowered leadership team member and other participants contributing what they do best.
- Responsibility is shared.
- Those closest to the person or group being served—in our case, the students—are supported by the full system embracing the same central goal and purpose.

This is not to say there isn't an ultimate leader. But enlightened leaders know when and how to loosen the reins and trade ego and control for the greater organizational good. Talented leaders know how to spot and nurture potential leaders from all levels to build a diversified leadership team that can handle the task of keeping teachers and staff motivated, supported, and focused on the end goal.

Element 5: Give Teaching the Professionalism It Deserves

I believe it's time we view teaching as a profession, and it's time that teachers think of themselves as professionals, the same way that a consultant or a scientist does. Professionals get, deserve, and need holistic professional development programs. Teachers deserve the same.

Evaluation has become a loaded word in education. This is the result of too many evaluation programs that exist in isolation; it's the consequence of evaluations that assess only the most basic functions of teachers. If evaluations are going to improve teacher performance, they must be part of a larger professional and talent management system, where the goal is to evaluate teachers against the broader desired result of student-centered learning.

While the purpose of evaluations should not be merely to call out ineffective instruction, every organization has employees whose performance needs improvement. Education is no different. However, in most cases, I see poor educator performance as a function of how little attention is given to them.

One of the main points of value in evaluating teachers comes in finding those teachers who are struggling and then identifying the reason why. But then what? Evaluations must be balanced by a support program in which teachers know they won't be shamed for weak performance, but instead provided the opportunity and tools to improve.

It's time to broaden our evaluation systems into full-scale, ongoing, professional development programs, where all staff is reviewed against clearly defined and articulated metrics, and a support structure is in place to help those struggling to meet improvement benchmarks. Under such a program, teachers and staff are far more likely to feel like they are achieving their own professional goals, which will keep motivation and morale high.

A professional development program planned with the desired end results in mind will also serve as an excellent lens through which to evaluate potential employees. Knowing you are hiring people who fit the culture of high expectations, who demonstrate the capacity to work toward evaluation standards, and who have the confidence to take support when needed will preclude talent issues in the longer run.

Element 6: Harness the Power of Data

We are living in the age of "big data." Data is everywhere. Data is more collectible than ever, it's more trackable than ever, it's more available than ever. And it can be more overwhelming than ever. Parsing data often requires analytics tools, and understanding it can require statistical expertise and some sort of training. It's the role of organizational leadership to recognize where and which analytics tools can be of benefit and provide any necessary training around how to turn data into insights and then insights into actionable plans.

My team and I have worked with several rapidly improving schools that have figured out how to cull data to inform decisions. I've seen several different data tools work. It's important to vet options and find the right solution for your district or school. It's the application of that tool that counts.

My team and I have identified seven common practices that rapidly improving schools apply for effective data use.

1. **Gather reflective student and performance data**. In the effort to use data for the ultimate goal of improved student performance, you must start with where you are. Valuable reflective data will include achievement measures—a student's performance at a point in time, or output—and progress measures—how much growth a student demonstrates over time, or outcome.

2. **Gather predictive data**. Once reflective data is gathered to paint a composite picture, it must be used to project the possible trajectory of each student. Forecasting will inform things like what resources or remedial programs might—or might not—be needed. In turn, this will help build staffing, budgeting, and capital resource need plans.

3. **Unify the information infrastructure**. The data collection and review process has to be streamlined and approachable—or else it will scare people off. It's up to organizational leadership to find and implement an accessible system.

4. **Decentralize reporting and access**. Data has to get into all rightful hands, or there's no point in it at all. The most successful data systems are easy-to-use, full-scale, web-based solutions accessible to administrators, teachers, parents, and students.

5. **Analyze the data**. Data is just data. Remember, the next step is determining insights that can be turned into action plans. Software and models can analyze data, and so too can humans. By asking probing questions, honest discussion can reveal root causes behind data results. What organizational leaders need to

remember is that teachers' plates are often too full to conduct analyses themselves.

6. **Use the data!** Data analysis is just data analysis. The ultimate point of data is to use it. Data insights can inform decisions around, to name a few uses, professional development; identifying teachers for mentor or leadership roles; implementing strategic staffing; evaluating program effectiveness and resource allocation; implementing strategic student course placement; and evaluating effectiveness of teachers and leadership.

7. **And finally, commit and communicate.** Communicate your commitment to data-driven decisions regularly to your stakeholders. When it comes to data, transparency and openness are the gateway to achieving maximal benefit from data.

Getting the most out of data, as you can tell, has to be a cooperative, inclusive process. It's most powerful when data-driven decision making is considered a core feature of the culture of high expectations.

Revolutionaries Get Killed

A final thought on implementing the elements of organizational leadership. *Make it voluntary.* I know that might not sit well with some, but allow me to build the case. Central administration can cause a lot of damage if it tries to *mandate* a culture change or a vision. Here's why: just about any staff can be broken into thirds. The top third loves change. They are the enthusiastic, eager, and zealous lot of early adopters who've never met a concept or new idea they didn't want to try. The middle third takes a "wait and see approach." They are cautious, thoughtful, and curious, but not willing to stick their necks out too far. The bottom third is adamantly resistant to change and finds comfort in the familiar and the known.

As administrators, how do you market change to three very different segments with three very different sets of desires, concerns, and values? I would urge you to consider making change *voluntary*. There's nobody more impatient about changing schools than me, but I've also learned this nugget of wisdom over the years: *Revolutionaries get killed.* You must be *evolutionary* in your approach. If you try to change too quickly, the bottom third will tell the middle third that this too will pass, just like every other failed initiative from the past three decades.

Start with that top third who love change. As administrators, your role here is to throw your limited professional development dollars and your limited discretionary money at this group. Get them more training. Give them maximum support. Don't worry about anyone else.

Eventually the top third will buy in and start convincing the middle third, and pretty soon you'll have two-thirds of your staff on board. But don't rush it; a process like this can't succeed in a year. It takes time. It takes a lot of work. It takes patient commitment. But if you get the culture right, and if you get the vision right, you've accomplished the hardest part.

The Story of Central Dauphin School District

When the Central Dauphin Board of Education named Dr. Carol Johnson as the district's new superintendent in 2012, it was planning to furlough 84 employees, cut programs, and raise taxes 3.3 percent to cover state-mandated pension contributions and an exploding expense budget. Welcome, Dr. Johnson!

Central Dauphin is a sprawling community of 86,000 just northeast of Harrisburg in south central Pennsylvania. The school district covers 118.2 square miles and is comprised of three boroughs and four townships. The student population of 10,000-plus is spread out in 13 elementary schools, four middle schools, and two high schools. The student poverty rate ranges from 20 percent to 40 percent. Students speak 38 different languages and more than 500 are enrolled in English as a second language (ESL).

Johnson was no stranger to Central Dauphin. She joined the district in 1998, first as assistant principal at Central Dauphin High School for five years. She went on to become principal at one of the middle schools for four years and then returned to Central Dauphin High School for three years as principal.

Today the district is two years into what Johnson calls the RRR Initiative—a plan to emphasize rigor, relevance, and relationships at every point. "We are trying to stress high rigor and high relevance across the board, from kindergarten to twelfth grade," she says. "We want kids to think critically when they leave here. We want to make sure kids get the skills that will get them the jobs that we don't even know exist yet.

"If you are trying to hit a moving target like that, we think you give kids the best chance to succeed by teaching them to be exceptional readers, exceptional writers, and not afraid to do some mathematics. It's a work in progress but we're getting there, we're beginning to see a change in the culture."

In Her Own Words: Dr. Carol Johnson

Johnson has been superintendent of Central Dauphin School District in Pennsylvania since 2012. She joined the district in 1998, first as an assistant principal, then as principal.

Tell us a little bit about the district and community.

The district is huge! But it's not a community in the same sense that a town is; it's not tightly knit at all. On one side of the district, we have a very high poverty rate, and on the other side, I would say we have a medium poverty rate. The biggest challenge we face as a district is the belief by parents on the high poverty side that their schools are treated inequitably, and that the more affluent area siphons off all the resources. It's actually the opposite. Since I became superintendent, the biggest thing I've tried to do is to dispel this myth about a lack of equity. The good thing is that the schools are very tightly knit and the relationships are strong. I think the teachers and the kids do a great job with what they have.

Tell us about the RRR Initiative.

I started attending professional development programs focused on leadership. Through one, I heard Bill Daggett speak. He spoke about the urgent need for students to get a rigorous and relevant experience in school. This just resonated with me because I believe that regardless of whether kids are in a high-poverty or low-poverty school, there are many students in those buildings who need more. It's that old expression—a rising tide lifts all ships. We believed that if we brought Bill in to speak to our district about rigor, relevance, and relationships, it would hit a chord with our teachers, and that's exactly what happened. The teachers believed we needed to do something very much along the lines of what Bill was talking about. So we started to design some professional development programs, and I started engaging our school board. We knew it was going to cost nearly $3 million over four years to build a really sustained program. Somehow I convinced the board to do it, and here we are. They believed then, and they still believe.

We are trying to stress high rigor and high relevance across all grades. We want kids to think critically when they leave here. We want kids to be much better readers, much better writers, and much better thinkers because we believe literacy and numeracy will get them the jobs of the future.

The only way we know to do that is to take our teachers, develop them into leaders, and also teach them how to get through to kids living in this century. As I keep telling them, the twentieth century ended 15 years ago, and here you are still doing the same things in the same ways. That really got their attention.

Has everyone bought into the program?

We certainly can't get every last person, but even so, we do have incredible buy-in. Our approach is that we're going to train our best teachers, and they in turn will train the others. We'll keep pushing this down the pipeline until we build capacity throughout the district. We do have some naysayers, but some of them are beginning to say, "If she can do it, I can do it."

Discuss your leadership style.

I want this fixed yesterday! But I believe we've put together an administrative team that is really a team—we are so like-minded. I use a very collaborative approach; it's kind of like a scrum when we are problem solving. We're all in this one room kicking the ball around and around, but by the time we walk out of there we are one mind, one voice. Sure we have bad days when you just want to burst into tears. But when I think I can't do this for one more minute, I'll get an email from a teacher thanking me for helping her change and for helping to make her a better teacher. And I'll go running down the hall passing out copies of that email to everyone I see. Then we regroup, go home, and start all over again the next day.

Are you starting to see success?

Not necessarily in the numbers or in the test scores, but we are seeing a profound change with the teaching staff. They understand that the things they've learned make their jobs a little easier, and the kids really respond to these new approaches. They also are eager to help teach their colleagues how to begin to master these changes. That kind of change is monumental. Change is happening, slowly and steadily.

Discuss the role of central administration.

It's critical, absolutely critical. In this district, there is no autopilot for central administration. We could have easily said to the staff, "You're going to do this," and then sat back and munched our doughnuts and answered our email and moved on to making sure all the toilets flushed. But we are at this every single day, speaking with one voice. If we were hands off—as we were with every other failed initiative in the past— we would have never gotten to where we are now in such a short time. It's all about the vision we have, making sure we do the groundwork, supporting the systems around us, and never, ever climbing out of the trenches.

What about the role of the Learning Criteria?

The Learning Criteria is at the heart of all the changes we are trying to make here. For us, it's really about the whole child. We have to move beyond this obsession with standardized test scores. We've got to allow kids to seek out and experience opportunities that are greater than learning how to read, write, and calculate. We need to give the kids the ultimate sense of belonging and accomplishment in school, to build a culture where learning is cool and learners are honored for their achievements.

We realize that schools are a refuge for a lot of these kids. It's a place where we can challenge and nurture them every day. This is their ticket out and we need them to see that this is where they begin and began to meet their life potential. We own these kids for seven-and-a-half hours a day, and if I can get them here, I have at least a fighting chance of making them successful.

Any final thoughts?

Let me go back to standardized testing. Yes, right now we're enduring criticism from the public for some of our results, but to us these kids are not numbers. They come to us with incredible challenges, and it's our job to fix every single one of their challenges. What we're trying to do is get them ready to pass the biggest test of all—being successful in life. That's the test that matters most to us.

Chapter Seven

A Closer Look: Instructional Leadership

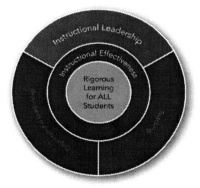

Sharon R. Wolder has figured out how to stay focused on what's important while simultaneously juggling urgent crises, which surface daily at Massachusetts' largest high school.

"You always seem to be drinking out of a fire hose," says Wolder, the principal of Brockton High School. "The other day I walked in the door and we had a floor that was completely flooded. Your attitude has to be, 'All right, let's get that taken care of and then we'll move on to the next thing.'

"But you have to stay focused on what we need to do to make sure kids are learning. [As a principal,] you constantly check to see what's happening in the classroom, and you constantly try to figure out what people need and make sure they get what they need. It gets back to that concept of principal as instructional leader."

What's Important Versus What's Urgent

If you are a building principal, you're dealing with figurative fire alarms all day long. The number of crises on any given day consumes you, and you develop a tendency to get caught up in the *urgent* at the expense of the *important*. If you're Sharon Wolder, you're managing about 4,200 kids and about 365 educators. How, for example, does she make sure her math teachers are providing a more engaging curriculum, while at the same time dealing with online bullying or a turkey running through the halls? Principals face issues like this daily.

Leading by Walking Around

"When you take on the job of principal, you commit yourself to very long hours," Wolder says. "But that's OK because you want people to know that you're in the building, and you want people to know that the school is safe, and you want people to know that when problems arise, those problems will be taken care of."

A native of Iowa, Wolder joined the staff of Brockton as a student teacher in 1994. In 1995, the school promoted her to history teacher, and she was off and running. In 2002, she was named social science department head, and from 2004 to 2010, she served as housemaster to one of the school's buildings. Then in 2010, she took over as Associate Principal of Curriculum and Instruction and was promoted to principal in 2013.

"You want people to see you. You want them to know that your focus is what's happening in the classroom, which is why I visit them on a regular basis. I simply get out of my office and I walk. I tell teachers I'm interested in what they're doing, but I'm really more interested in what the students are doing. That's because students' level of engagement tells me that they are, in fact, learning. If they can't explain what they are doing, then we have a problem, and we need to find ways to get that teacher some help."

Element 1: Raise the Bar for Learning and Instruction

Instructional leaders deal with a high degree of ambiguity. But no matter the unexpected distractions put in front of them, ultimately they must remain steadfastly focused on what matters most: galvanizing everyone around a vision for high student achievement.

How do you create a school culture of high expectations focused on rigor, relevance, and relationships, especially in an urban school like Brockton with high poverty, unemployment, and foreclosure rates? How do you engage those students?

The key is motivation. Most students are either motivated or obedient. The obedient student is the kid who comes to school and does whatever the teacher asks him or her to do. If you are an adult, an obedient student is a delight to be around. But then there are those like a couple of my grandsons who need to see school as relevant in order to be motivated to do well. Why do I have to go to school? What's in it for me? Why do I need to do this? At schools like Brockton, a majority of kids need to be motivated if they are going to learn.

Children of poverty often lack the supportive environment that contributes to academic success. Teachers may mistake low performance with lack of ability and therefore not hold these students to the same standards as other students.

We researched high-poverty schools where the majority of students were achieving at high levels, like at Brockton. What made these schools so effective in closing the achievement gap? We identified several factors, but one stood out in particular.

There was—and remains—a shared belief in and commitment to the concept that *all students will achieve*. In other words, these schools have high expectations for ALL students, no matter a student's circumstances. This attitude is prevalent throughout and surfaces in school mission statements, communications, student work, and academic awards. Most importantly, this attitude is evident in conversations with all school staff and students. Leadership also regularly uses reports, studies, and data to reinforce the idea that every last student is capable of achieving to his or her highest potential under the appropriate learning conditions. Despite setbacks, effective teachers persist in their bedrock belief that ALL students can learn. It takes a shared vision and a clearly articulated and communicated plan for change to reach that goal. From there you build strategies, programs, and activities that reinforce the culture and help children rise to the high expectations set for them.

The Rigor/Relevance Framework®

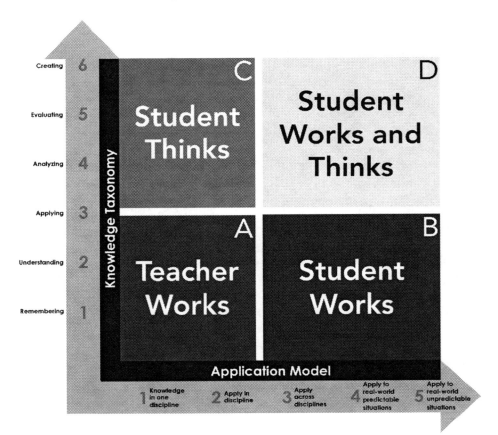

The Rigor/Relevance Framework is a powerful tool through which we can measure all instruction. The Framework raises expectations for how teachers teach so that students are given the tools needed to meet high expectations. Using rigor and relevance as a reference, we can see that the most useful preparation for students to enter the world of work—and to succeed in new state assessments—happens in Quadrant D. Yet most testable material resides in Quadrant A. We find that most schools—especially high schools—teach in Quadrants B and C. The college prep program is an example of Quadrant C, with strong academics but often little relevance to the real world. An example of Quadrant B is career and technical education, which teaches real-world applications of basic academic knowledge, but not at an especially rigorous level.

Quadrants A and C focus on acquisition, storing, and skillful retrieval of knowledge, but Quadrants B and D prepare students for the real world—and that's where we want to devote most attention.

How do you get there? You start thinking about creating an interdisciplinary curriculum.

Element 2: Align the Vision to Standards Through Interdisciplinary Curriculum

Schools traditionally organize curriculum by putting subjects into silos. That's a huge problem because the real world doesn't function in disciplines. We took what kids needed to know in math and we put all that content into one silo. What do they need to know about English language arts? We'll put that in another silo. Social studies and history? Separate silo. Then we go out and hire teachers to teach the content in these silos. Do you see what we've done? We've let subject specific standards drive curriculum and organized our schools to make it easier for the teachers to teach. But that's not how students use information. As students move from class to class, they are exposed to isolated bits of knowledge, but they seldom learn how information in one class relates to another—and they certainly don't learn how this knowledge applies to the world outside of school. We have a huge organizational problem—and it puts how teachers teach first and how students learn last.

We've developed rules, regulations, certification, tenure, and contracts that reinforce individual disciplines. A math teacher can't teach science because she's not certified to do it.

What an instructional leader must do is figure out how to bend those rules, regulations, certifications, tenure, and contracts so that they fit into the vision, not the other way around. In other words, they must take control, not be controlled. That's the only way you can introduce relevant instruction to your students. Schools need to move from a curriculum built around single disciplines to an interdisciplinary curriculum. This will require substantial effort, support systems, and time. Schools cannot just flip a switch and make it happen. Remember, significant change like this has to be evolutionary.

A strong principal can start to introduce an interdisciplinary approach by enlisting the school's top teachers. This is where a principal as "instructional leader" is so critical. The key is for the principal to find teachers from different disciplines who like and respect each other. From there, the principal should ask these teachers to begin planning an interdisciplinary curriculum together. Eventually, these mini-teams of "friends" will encourage others to join forces. Slowly but surely, an interdisciplinary approach will begin to spread to more and more teachers, until it is the predominant curriculum strategy. Too often, principals try to force teachers together; success comes when teachers are allowed to partner with people they enjoy working with and the work feels fun.

The next focus is on the master schedule, which lays out who teaches which courses and when. To begin building a new, interdisciplinary schedule, start first with those teams of friends from different disciplines and prioritize their scheduling needs. Then schedule everyone else. The end result, and the end goal, is to structure the schedule so that what a teacher teaches in first period math relates to second period science, which relates to third period English, and so on. You could even take it a step farther and make sure these teachers have the same prep period so they can talk and plan—a simple tactic that doesn't cost anything.

Seven Questions

Developing any curriculum involves much more than organizing content into a scope and a sequence. Instructional leaders, working with the teachers they support, need to answer the following questions to ensure that an interdisciplinary curriculum includes the necessary features.

1. **Standards**: What do students need to know and be able to do by grade level and course of study?
2. **Content knowledge**: What level of skill in applying that knowledge must students possess to ensure that they will succeed in future endeavors?
3. **Expectations**: What level of proficiency do we expect all students to achieve in each grade?
4. **Assessment practices**: How will student learning and achievement be measured?
5. **Structures**: Do existing structures, regulations, resources, tools, and physical surroundings need to be changed to support a goal of interdisciplinary instruction and learning?
6. **Effective instructional practices**: What levels of expertise and knowledge must every teacher master to help students achieve?
7. **The ability to help students connect applications to knowledge**: What do teachers and instructional leaders need to make learning more meaningful for students?

At the risk of being repetitive, these features of an aligned interdisciplinary curriculum should define and support student achievement. Also, by measuring curriculum against each of these points, schools can guarantee they remain in control of building a curriculum on vision, not external demands.

Culture Trumps Strategy

As I've often said, I believe you can divide school staff into thirds. The top third are the ones who've never met an innovation they didn't want to try. The middle third are cautious and thoughtful, but not sure they want to take a risk. The bottom third vows never to change.

In building an interdisciplinary curriculum, the instructional leader will start with the top third and then build the curriculum around them. Cut those teachers loose, and they'll make it work. And then the middle third will take notice and will begin to say, "Hey, you know what? That system is not bad at all. Ms. Principal, next year can I get involved in that?" And that's how you do it.

Culture trumps strategy. You create the culture and empower your staff to determine and work through the details of the strategy. But if you create the strategy first before you have created the culture, the newest strategy becomes the latest enemy.

Element 3: Integrate Literacy, Math, and Technology Across All Subjects

Think about the jobs that computers can do. They can do any sort of rote tasks, like process insurance claims or scan reams of legal briefs for particular words and data. Think about the jobs they can't do. They can't provide janitorial services or repair electrical wiring. They also can't find new cures to diseases or launch a company. In the Prologue, I described in depth the missing middle—the middle-class sector of the economy that is getting hollowed out by automation, artificial intelligence, and robotics, while simultaneously pushing more work to the lower and upper skill bounds.

The high-skill, high-paying jobs of the future will require literacy and the skills gained through mathematical thinking. And every student is going to need a solid grasp of how to navigate predominant technologies. Either we provide students with these skills and put them on a path toward productive, fruitful careers, or we don't and we relegate them to low-skill labor and a high likelihood of little to no self-sufficiency.

Both literacy and math are enabling skills: they make learning in other disciplines more accessible. Students who struggle with reading lack the means, and often the self-confidence, to achieve success in other areas. Many students do poorly in math not because they can't *do* the math, but because they can't *comprehend* the problems. Students are frequently turned off by social studies because their reading and writing skills are lacking. Others dislike science because they are threatened by the math in formulas and other calculations.

Math also supports the development of adaptive reasoning, strategic competence, conceptual understanding, procedural fluency, and productive disposition—all skills that students will need in the more complex, technology-driven, and well-paying careers.

All teachers, no matter their subject specialization, must make literacy, mathematical proficiency, and technological proficiency a top priority. Teachers specialized in subjects other than English language arts, math, or technology must find ways to incorporate these subjects into their courses where possible. By doing so, we will not only better prepare our students for success in college, careers, and adult life after high school, but also help them experience more success in a full range of other subjects and disciplines.

Element 4: Use Data to Inform Instruction

In Chapter Six, we looked at how organizational leadership can get the most out of data to inform most any decision. Here, we'll take a closer look at how to use data effectively for instructional improvements.

The key to culling instructional data is to measure it against your school's end goal. When using data to direct how and what you teach, it's crucial to ensure that data is connected to your desired results. For example, is this the right data to track to gain insights about how successfully we are merging subjects to teach a more interdisciplinary curriculum? Will this tool merely show us how well students are retaining knowledge, or will it show us how effectively they've learned to apply that knowledge to real-world scenarios?

The data you collect is only as useful as its ability to reveal your school's progress in meeting an objective. When you're using the appropriate data tools and analysis, they can be a powerful way to reveal—and then help you correct—teaching tactics that aren't serving your goals as effectively as anticipated or intended.

Element 5: Rethink Professional Development

A word about professional development. There are hundreds of courses, programs and seminars out there. But we have identified three areas of critical importance in terms of ongoing development, for both new and experienced teachers and administrators:

- **Rigor and Relevance:** Teachers need the ability to present concepts and problems to students in different ways, figure out where students have gone off the track, and make other in-class adjustments. Research shows that when teachers gain content knowledge or subject matter certification, it has a positive impact on student achievement in all subjects (Hattie, 2009), especially math. (Hill, Ball, and Rowan, 2005) This is because subject mastery increases a teacher's capacity to explain a topic from a variety of angles, apply it to real-world scenarios, recognize a student's confusion, and offer individualized clarifications.
- **Differentiated and Scaffolded Instruction:** Many teachers will need support to meet the needs of an increasingly diverse student population. Differentiating and scaffolding instruction can maximize growth for all students, especially those who have difficulty with reading. Teachers will need training to learn to assess all students' abilities and use this information to raise achievement for each of them on an individualized basis.
- **Leadership Development:** It should be ongoing and focused on student achievement. Leadership development also should be part of an aligned, long-range plan for school improvement. Finally, it should be planned in collaboration with teachers and leaders who want to participate.

In our experience, sustained and consistent professional learning programs that align with teacher evaluation systems are the most effective.

Tactics we've seen have great success are job-embedded professional development coaches who work with teachers in the classroom to guide them through instructional improvements. Developing a schoolwide habit of regularly adopting, adapting, and collaboratively implementing proven best practices is also highly effective. What's key is that any assessment tools used to ascertain the level of impact of any professional development initiative must measure both its impact on the teacher *and* the learner.

Ultimately, it is the job of instructional leadership to know what their teachers need to do their jobs more effectively, and then match them with the right professional development program to get them there. When teachers feel supported, then they can remain focused on putting students' needs first. When they don't, they get distracted by focusing too much attention on their own needs and interests, and then student achievement goals cannot be met.

Remember: begin with the end in mind. Are your colleagues the guardians of a twentieth century education system or the leaders of a twenty-first century system? The answer should be obvious.

Element 6: Get Parents and the Community Involved

When parents and communities engage in student learning, we see dramatic improvements in student achievement. These improvements tend to happen across the board, which helps begin to close the student achievement gap. It is for this reason that we've recently added this crucial element to the instructional leadership segment.

The challenge today is creating opportunities for meaningful engagement that appeal to a diverse set of parents. A lack of parent engagement can result from a host of reasons. More and more parents work full-time, leaving both parents with less time available for school involvement. More parents are not native English speakers and the language barrier might cause some discomfort around active and participatory school engagement. Just as teachers must find a way to teach to an increasingly diverse student body, schools must find a way to appeal to a diverse set of parents.

What we have found is that the schools with the most productive school–family relationships put engagement on the parents' terms, not the school's. They ask for parent involvement at times that work for the parents and make engagement as comfortable and convenient as possible. They host events or discussions at community centers, like firehouses or booster clubs, in an effort to be as accommodative as possible. They find ways to make non-native English speaking parents feel comfortable attending school events. We've seen schools have great success doing so by incorporating cultural programs into learning where parents are invited to watch or participate; this can be an excellent way to get some otherwise hesitant parents in the door, so to speak. Once they can see firsthand that their involvement is welcome, wanted, and comfortable, they will be more likely to continue to participate in the school community. When parents feel that their work demands, the pressure to support their families, and any cultural differences are acknowledged and respected, they are typically more inclined to carve out time for school involvement.

The most rapidly improving schools have also built creative parent engagement programs that go beyond PTA meetings or occasional parent-teacher conferences. Teachers might create a learning module on family heritage, where parents are asked to come in for one class to share with their child their family history. A range of volunteer opportunities for families can be devised, be it volunteering to come in and speak about their careers or helping out in a classroom session.

School engagement heightens stakeholder awareness and accountability. When families are exposed to how their children are learning, they naturally feel a reflexive desire to ensure a school is acting in accordance with their children's best interests. And they feel more motivated to do what's necessary to help their children achieve.

Communities are also stakeholders in student achievement; after all, it is these students who will one day take the community reins. Schools have a responsibility to convey this fact to encourage community support in providing students a rigorous and relevant education so that they can become responsible bearers of their local community. Community engagement also makes students feel broadly supported;

this is necessary in itself, but can also help, to some degree, offset instances where parents cannot or are not lending support.

Rapidly improving schools reach out to local businesses, government agencies, specialized organizations, and cultural institutions to find opportunities to collaborate. Business leaders can teach mini-career academies. An employee from an art museum can team up with a history teacher to lead a class session on how art from a specific period served as an outlet of protest. A local government official can join the math teacher in explaining how surveys and statistics are used to collect and analyze local demographic data to inform policy decisions.

When students can directly tie learning to their local worlds, not only are they seeing how skills relate to careers, but they also begin to appreciate the importance and reward of being citizens who make positive contributions to their communities.

In Her Own Words: Sharon R. Wolder

Wolder has worked at Brockton High School in Brockton, Mass., since arriving as a student teacher in 1994. She was promoted to principal in 2013.

You were a member of the Restructuring Committee at Brockton that developed the highly successful Literacy Initiative. What was that experience like?

I was excited to be on the committee. At that time, we were one of the worst-performing high schools in Massachusetts. We were dealing with a lot of issues: the dropout rate was high, the failure rate was high. Nothing seemed to be working, and so the committee's mission was to find ways to turn things around. Most of us believed things could get better. We hit some bumps along the way—we were trying to outguess the MCAS assessment test, for example, which was the wrong approach. We finally went back and looked at what our kids were being asked to do. We started looking at what skills they were being asked to use and what skills they needed in order to answer the questions on the test. Our conversation turned from *What is going to be on the test?* to *What do our students need to be able to do when they graduate or are ready to go out into the world of work?* The answer was reading, writing, speaking, and reasoning—literacy, in other words. But not everyone in the school agreed. When we spread the message to the entire school, there was a group of people who wanted to change and a group of people who didn't. It was tough to listen to so much negativity, but we made sure everyone had a voice and everyone was heard. In the end, we developed a culture that spread schoolwide and continues to this day.

What are your views on using technology in the classroom?

We have incorporated technology in a lot of different ways and will continue to do so. But it's sometimes a struggle. We have some teachers who are reluctant to open email, and some who are comfortable designing web pages. There's a huge gap. We have to meet teachers where they are and help them take the next step. Our students know how to use technology. Our goal is to make sure they are using technology appropriately. That's why digital literacy is so critical for us.

How do you handle the pressures of the job?

Well, you have to deal with the crises. You have to keep the school safe and running, otherwise instruction can't happen. That is a priority. But some days are so much harder than others. I've found that you have to be good at calmly reacting to things; you just have to go into a solving mode.

How do you handle staff members who resist change?

Those are some of the best conversations you can have with someone—as long as you don't make it personal. At some point in my career I took a neurology class, and it was the best thing I could have done. You learn about fear and how people respond when they are angry or apprehensive. So when a teacher tells me, "I don't want to do this," I will eventually ask this question: "What are you afraid of?" You are trying to get people to the point where they can admit to their fears and acknowledge them. But you can't ever make it personal. You acknowledge their fears, but then try to convince them that if it is the right thing to do for students, then it's worth trying. You just have to make sure the teachers who struggle the most get the most support, while at the same time still hold everyone accountable.

What goals do you have as principal at Brockton?

Obviously, I hope we maintain our high academic standards. We also have to get ready for new assessments and make sure our teachers get the support they need to provide this next level of instruction. I believe strongly that our students should be actively involved in community service. That's important to me. Students need to connect to the community they live in, and they need to do things that are not about themselves. It's all about making where they live a better place. We have real needs in our community, so I tell students to do something that matters. You never get to where you're going alone—somebody always helps you along. You have to be decent enough to help somebody else. That's an important lesson to learn.

Any final thoughts?

There are no classes you can take that teach you how to be a good principal. I've learned that you just have to connect with good people. You have to learn how to work with others and learn how to build a team. At the same time, you have to walk in your own shoes and walk on your own path. It's all about the relationships you make with other people. If you do it sincerely and honestly, they will help you, which makes your job so much easier.

References

Hattie, John (2009). *Visible learning: A synthesis of over 800 meta-analyses relating to achievement.* New York: Routledge.

Hill, Heather C., Deborah Loewenberg Ball, and Brian Rowan (2005). "Effects of teachers' mathematical knowledge for teaching on student achievement." *American Education Research Journal*, 42(2), 371–406.

Chapter Eight

A Closer Look: Teaching

We have a tendency to obsess about the latest trend. The buzz today is organizational leadership, which we discussed two chapters ago. Ten years ago it was instructional leadership, which we discussed in the last chapter. But let's not forget what we know. Yes, organizational leadership and instructional leadership are important, but nothing is more important than teaching. Teaching is still what this is all about.

In the 1980s, I was in the New York State Department of Education leading a new initiative we called Futuring. The philosophy behind Futuring was that we needed to look to the future and move away from the past as we made decisions about education. The new courses we developed from that initiative were controversial, especially with teachers' unions. Some teachers went after me with a vengeance.

Why were they so upset? Because, as I explained in Chapter Two, they weren't prepared to teach the new courses called Principles of Technology, Home/Career Skills, Introduction to Occupations, Information Systems, and Financial Management. The courses emphasized teaching employable skills that would not become obsolete as society and technology evolved. These courses pushed teachers out of their comfort zones. They simply didn't know what students needed to compete successfully for future—and not yet known—jobs and careers.

Back then, everyone involved in education reform focused on teaching. We understood that what happens between teacher and student is critical. Since then, we've learned that teachers need support at the building level and from central administration. But in the end, it's still all about teaching.

A Seismic Shift

In almost every speech I give, I ask this series of questions:

> *All you fourth grade teachers, raise your hands. What are you supposed to be getting your students ready for? That's right, fifth grade! And the purpose of elementary school is to get kids ready for—that's right, middle school! And the purpose of middle school is to get students ready for high school! And high school is supposed to get students ready for college!*

Then I pause.

> *And then these students fall off the educational ladder or graduate from college and return home to mom and dad because they're mostly unemployable.*

There is stunned, uncomfortable silence.

Today, I believe the role of teaching is undergoing a seismic shift. Today, the role of a teacher isn't simply to impart knowledge and prepare students for the next grade. Instead, *teachers must teach students how to use knowledge.*

It's not just about rigor; it's about rigor, relevance, and the relationships that enable relevance. *Relevance makes rigor possible.*

Overworked, Over-Stressed

On our journey to rigor and relevance, we often run into a major problem: we're adding more and more to teachers' plates. Teaching is more stressful today than it's ever been. Teachers' stress levels are off the charts and demands on their time are greater than ever—but their pay grades do not take this into account.

The problem lies in the way we've organized schools. It's not the fault of the teachers—they are just trying to function within the system. Most schools are operating in the A and C quadrants of the Rigor/ Relevance Framework. If you want to move students into the B and D quadrants, you can't do it one discipline at a time. As a result, you've got incredible stress on a structure that was organized in the twentieth century. We've got rules, regulations, certification, tenure, and contracts all geared to the A and C side. To move students to the B and D side, teachers must find ways to break down the old, outdated organizational structure and build a new one.

Element 1: Rigor and Relevance for Every Last Student

As demands and stress on teachers increase, a disturbing trend is underway: the teacher is doing all the work—and students are sitting back and watching. In too many classrooms, education has become a spectator sport where teachers struggle to move through all the requirements while students sit passively, sometimes bored and checked out. When teachers are too overwhelmed with managing and disseminating information, they lack the time to make learning relevant to each student. When outside demands dictate learning, the focus on rigor and relevance for ALL necessarily takes second place, at best.

If we want students to function in the real-world quadrants of B and D, the role of the teacher must change. Rather than being a disseminator of knowledge, the teacher must become more of a facilitator, transitioning from the so-called "sage on the stage" to a "guide from the side." From this mindset and approach, teachers naturally give each student individual care and attention, which is critical to helping all students find the confidence to rise to meet high and rigorous expectations.

Good examples of teachers who often make students feel highly cared for and believed in are athletic coaches. The coach–student relationship puts the coach in the role of vital supporter in the student's active engagement. Baseball or football coaches are not playing the game; the kids are. The coaches get their players to "do." They also encourage real-world skills like teamwork, leadership, honesty, self-discipline, communication, collaboration, mutual respect, and peer support. For many students, coaches are the "go-to" adults at school with whom they share their personal issues and confidences. It's no coincidence that sports are the main reason many students attend school.

Let me share another story about our son, Paul. After years of rehabilitation and physical therapy after the accident, Paul was ready for ninth grade. When he came home after the first day of classes, he told us he would be late getting home the next day. When we asked why, his answer stunned us: "The cross-country coach told me he wants me on the team."

My wife and I were flabbergasted. Paul could hardly walk. We knew Paul must have misunderstood the coach. We decided to find out what was going on. It turned out that yes, the coach had asked Paul to join the team. "What's most important to me," the coach said, "is that *all* of my runners *improve every day.*"

Paul ran for all four years of high school and never finished better than last. But that didn't matter; he improved. He continuously beat his previous best time. His experience on the team helped Paul re-engage with school. The coach helped Paul believe in himself. Is there anything more important than that?

Element 2: The Third R: Build a Relationship-Based Learning Environment

While we know relevance makes rigor possible, we too often forget that what is relevant to one student may not be relevant to the next. Relevance is a very personal thing.

So how do we know what is relevant to a student? By developing close relationships with all students. The third R—relationships—is the key to being able to enable a student to complete a rigorous and relevant curriculum. It is also key to teaching the whole child and addressing personal, social, and emotional needs as well. Strong teacher–student bonds have been shown to build a trust that positively impacts learners and the learning environment.

This all may sound daunting and overwhelming. But it might also be helpful to know that this sort of 3Rs teaching surrounds us. We have several role models to which we can look for guidance in learning how to make the 3Rs the fulcrum of our instruction.

- Special education teachers: Teachers who work with students with disabilities use approaches that all teachers must begin to adopt. They know their students well. They establish strong one-to-one relationships. They foster trust and mutual respect.
- Teachers who teach gifted students: The same applies here. These teachers know their students well and recognize that their students are outside the mainstream for learning potential. They actively engage students rather than just impart knowledge.
- Career and technical education teachers: The philosophy of these teachers is "learn to do" rather than "learn to know." These are hands-on instructors who reach their students through active learning.
- Fine arts teachers: They recognize and cultivate interest and talent in music, drama, dance, sculpture, painting, and the visual arts. Because artistic self-expression is so personal, teachers often develop close, trusting relationships with students. They are able to recognize, appreciate, encourage, and nurture emerging talent.

- Counselors, tutors, and advisers: Through some form of personalized instruction, they interact closely with students to coach and guide them to new understanding or mastery.
- Other students: Many schools use senior students to tutor or coach younger students. For example, the program *Learning Together* enlists older at-risk students to tutor younger at-risk students. The program focuses on reading skills, ostensibly for the younger student, but both students benefit. These students often develop relationships that extend beyond the tutoring sessions.

One Approach: Looping

How else could we help our stressed-out, overwhelmed teachers build stronger relationships with all students? By looping.

The practice of looping—where a teacher moves to the next grade with her students instead of sending them to a new teacher—has been successfully used in Europe for years. But looping is rare in this country. Looping has several key advantages, including:

- A stronger bond between teachers and students, students and students, and even parents and teachers
- Greater understanding of students' strengths and weaknesses, which allows teachers to tailor curriculum to individual needs
- Greater support for students who need stabilizing influences in their lives
- Increased opportunities for students to develop self-confidence
- Reduced anxiety about the new school year

To be fair, looping sometimes can backfire due to:

- A bad fit between student and teacher
- The possibility of struggling with a poor teacher for several years
- Less exposure to new students and teaching styles

Still, I believe the more we can loop, the better off we will be. Most teachers spend almost an entire year getting to really know their students well—and then they are gone.

Element 3: Put Content in a Relevant Context

We asked students at high-poverty, high-achieving schools what teachers did best to help them learn. The answers from virtually every student were the same: The teacher cares about me and knows something personal about me. The teacher has rules but is fair, knows the subject matter, uses a variety of learning activities, and makes learning interesting and fun.

Almost every student described his or her best learning experience as an action-oriented lesson with real-world context. For example, learning how plants grow by visiting a greenhouse, using math to measure the height of a flagpole without climbing it, making scale maps of the neighborhood, or learning about checking and savings accounts on a field trip to a bank.

To pull off this sort of consistent real-world learning, teachers must put time and effort into staying on top of the latest and most effective pedagogy, the most contemporary content, and the types of experiences to connect back to that content that will resonate most with students. Expert subject knowledge remains essential; the more mastery teachers have on a subject, the more they can pose thoughtful questions, address misconceptions, help students see points from multiple angles, and guide students toward critical thinking. Twenty-first century teaching requires that teachers take deep subject knowledge a bit further and put it into a larger context that is interesting to their students, and this is achieved through continual teacher learning.

All teachers should put up this sign in front of their classrooms: "Where will I ever use what you're teaching me today?" We should always tell students *why* they need to know the material and strategies we're teaching, and the reason should never be, "To get you ready for next year."

A Caveat on Context

The classroom is no place for ideology. When looking for real-world context to support content, check your politics at the door. If we teach point of view, we rob our students of the crucial lesson of learning to think critically and independently. In today's digital, information overloaded, globalized world, those are practically survival skills.

Consider all of the information available on the Internet, where we are bombarded with questionable or fraudulent sources of information all the time. Even our so-called trusted sources of information can raise eyebrows. Just consider how differently MSNBC and Fox News can report on the same story. We have a responsibility to help students learn how to vet information through a discerning lens. The role of a teacher is to not to tell students *what* to think about information, but *how* to think critically about it.

Element 4: A Toolkit for Strategic Instruction

Why do some teachers connect with students while others don't?

In some cases, the answer may be that a teacher's teaching style is out of sync with how today's students learn. Recall my grandmother from Chapter Two who taught students in the early part of the twentieth century? Imagine how ill-equipped she'd be if she were dropped into a classroom today. Imagine even how ill-equipped your grade school teachers would be if they were dropped into a modern classroom. Without context, relevance is impossible.

Thanks to a multitude of new studies, our understanding of how people learn is growing exponentially. We are beginning to understand that today's students are "wired" differently from previous generations. Today's students typically need a reason to learn, and they take for granted instant access to information. They are digital natives. They multi-task. They collaborate naturally and seamlessly. And most importantly, they "do to learn" rather than "learn to do."

How our students learn today is simply different from how we learned, before technology infiltrated every aspect of life. To reach today's students, highly effective teachers put time and effort into building and maintaining a toolkit of strategic and research-based approaches that maximize mental stimulation and cooperative learning. Technology must be incorporated wherever possible, if even just as a tool to access all relevant course material, to match the habits of our twenty-first-century students and the skills they will need in the future. Teachers can also use technology behind the scenes: there are several technological tools that can help teachers manage classroom data and student feedback so that they can make more informed instruction decisions. Teachers can also use technology behind the scenes; there are several technological tools that can help teachers manage classroom data and student feedback so that they can make more informed instruction decisions. Data-driven and research-based best practices can be powerful tactics to bridge content and instruction. Developing a habit and a plan to refresh best practices as standards and content needs change will make for a well-rounded toolkit.

Teachers also have the difficult task of teaching to a diverse student body. This is no small feat, and it is achievable only through strategic instruction. Teachers must regularly seek and apply strategic instruction that *meets today's students' needs* and treats students as active learners rather than young people who sit in class and absorb knowledge. Lectures are out. Relying simply and exclusively on memorization is out. To connect with every student, the classroom must become a place where students work and teachers observe—not the other way around.

Based on new findings in our work with rapidly improving districts and schools, we've added two new points to this element: culturally relevant teaching and frequent, active family engagement. Culturally relevant teaching serves three aims. First, tying instruction to culture helps build a sense of community, which broadens the sense of support a student feels from the community and deepens the sense of responsibility he or she has to it. Second, when teachers think in terms of each student's culture and primary language, they will think in terms of any language acquisition support a student may need. Through purposeful awareness of a student's possible language barriers, a teacher can individualize learning to help that student overcome specific language or vocabulary challenges. Third, culturally relevant teaching opens up opportunities for parents whose first language is not English to feel comfortable in and integral to school engagement.

Family engagement has a direct and positive correlation on student achievement. In fact, it's so proven across multiple studies that it would be self-defeating not to take advantage of the rewarding endeavor to involve families in school, so long as their engagement is carried out in a way that is convenient and comfortable to them.

Exposure to knowledge may often happen in a classroom. But students—and all people—come to grasp and retain that knowledge by processing it through the world and experiences that have shaped how they think and learn. When we educators fail to understand the worlds students live in, we fail to reach them.

Element 5: Unlock the Power of Assessments to Improve Individualized Instruction

Dr. Gregory M. McGough is a tenth grade English teacher at Penn Manor High School in Millersville, Penn., and also an International Center consultant. McGough is a huge believer in the Rigor/Relevance Framework and applies it in every class he teaches. He's known for setting high expectations for every last student he teaches and for his commitment to ensuring each student rises to meet those expectations.

To confirm that all of his students are keeping pace with his rigorous teaching, McGough employs a unique kind of formative assessment to "grade" his students. "Kids can go back and redo their work as many times as they want until they have mastered the subject," he says.

"Kids say one of the things they like about me is that I'm encouraging, but I also hold them to a high level of rigor. I also give the kids a safety net, which is honesty. I'm never afraid to tell a student, 'No, actually you are not working hard and you don't know the material. You think you do, but you don't. What are we going to do about that?' I don't let them move on until they master the material."

Assessment data are the backbone to a rigorous and relevant curriculum. Why? Because they are the only way to determine if rigorous and relevant initiatives are delivering consistently on their aim to be rigorous and relevant. Tracking student progress, both during and at the end of instruction, will reveal to teachers where students are struggling. Strategic and appropriate assessments that align with learning objectives will give insight as to why. From there, teachers can amend instruction for each student based on his or her challenge spots. They can also advance teaching in cases where data reveals a student has already achieved mastery and is ready for more rigor.

Element 6: Rigorously, Faithfully, and Constantly Support Teachers

Let's take a moment to reflect on what we've asked teachers to do in this chapter. Raise expectations for ALL students and deliver instruction that empowers ALL students to meet these heightened expectations. Teach the whole child by addressing not only educational needs, but also emotional, personal, and social needs. Always update and refine content knowledge to link subject learning to real-world experiences that resonate with students. Keep on top of the latest research, best practices, technologies, and teaching strategies and integrate them into instruction. Engage families and the community. Track student progress over the short and long term and use data insights to inform differentiated teaching.

Did I mention teachers are overworked, overwhelmed, and over-stressed? Did I even need to?

Look. My aim here is *not* to further overwhelm teachers. Quite the opposite. The entire aim of this book is to provide a framework where every last person, from district office to school campus, is doing what he or she needs to do to provide teachers with the resources they need to do what they do best: teach. I'm trying to help teachers cut through the noise, the headaches, the external demands, and the distractions and leave them with a clear plan to update and reorganize their teaching to prepare students for the twenty-first century. My goal here is to help teachers regain control.

And here's the thing. I believe in our teachers. I know each and every last one is capable of rising to meet these new expectations for student-centered, twenty-first century instruction. But they can't do it alone. No one could.

Teachers need consistent support in continuous growth toward accessing and using best practices and the most effective strategies and integrating technology as often as possible. They also must have systemic support in an empowered, collaborative environment where they can take on leadership roles in the development and sharing of effective practices.

Only through a system that supports teacher development, collaboration, and professional growth will teachers gain the tools they need to be able to create learning environments that result in preparing ALL students for life and careers in the twenty-first century.

It takes everyone.

In His Own Words: Dr. Gregory M. McGough

McGough teaches English Language Arts at Penn Manor High School in Millersville, Penn. He is also a consultant for the International Center, specializing in technology and digital literacy.

You're a proponent of using technology in the classroom. What is your class like?

Every student in my class uses a laptop, so my classroom is mostly paperless. Everything is accessible to them on my website—every handout, every lesson plan, all the course material, everything they could possibly need—and it's available 24/7. Parents can also check in; they have up-to-the-minute access to everything their kids will be learning. We have complete and utter transparency. It's really powerful for my students because it allows them to learn when it's best for them.

We try different, innovative approaches. Back in March 2013, my class was reading *Lord of the Flies* at the time Malaysian Air Flight 370 disappeared. We decided to go to a crowd sourcing website called tomnod.com, where, in real time, you could search for the plane, debris, or even survivors. At one point, one of my students came up to me and said, "This is just like the book we're reading." It was one of those great moments—there we were, sitting in our classroom searching the Indian

Ocean for wreckage. That real-time exercise helped the kids relate to what they were reading.

When my students are reading nonfiction material, I sometimes use a video game to encourage them. The name of the game is Plague Inc., and the object is to create a virus and unleash it on the world. I have the kids read a book about diseases and their characteristics. After they finish reading, they play the game by recreating a virus and launching it. They can't beat the game unless they completely understand the signs and symptoms of diseases.

I discussed this approach at a conference once. After my presentation, a woman came up to me and told me I was creating a classroom of terrorists. When I explained that these kids just pored over some hard-to-understand material in an attempt to beat the game, she finally understood and thanked me. In each of these examples, the information my students were reading wasn't just material that would be on the next quiz, there's a real-world application to what they are doing. That's where relevance comes into it.

What strategies and practices have you used to create strong relationships with your students?

I meet with them weekly, every single student, every week. It gives us a chance to talk about their work and what's going on in their worlds. It also allows me to sit down with them and say, "OK, here's your grade. Now, what don't you understand? What can we do to make this better? What do you need from me to improve?" This approach allows me to set incredibly high standards. At the same time, all of my students know that I won't let them move on until they really understand the lesson.

I also share a lot of my own personal life—administrators sometimes tell teachers not to do this, but I do it because I know it works for me. I tell the kids my stories, and they ask questions. My kids know that I care about each and every one of them. There are no favorites in my class—everybody gets a fair shot.

We don't back away from any topic, but I do insist that there will be no bullying in my class. When you come into my room, we treat each other with respect. There's a certain elevation to our dialogue that you must have in order for students to feel comfortable and safe. I'm not trying to convince you one way or the other, but I do want you to come up with your own opinion. That one-on-one attention with each kid really seems to help. I tell them that one day in the future they might be sitting in a dorm room struggling with a problem, and I won't be anywhere around. They're going to have to figure out what to do on their own.

Part Three

The Daggett System for Effective Instruction: Best Practices

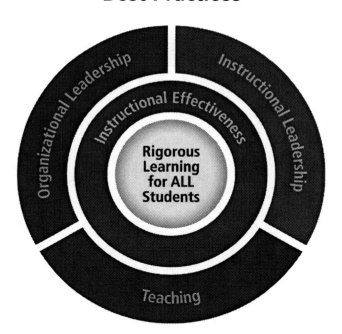

Best Practices: An Overview

Best practices, especially innovative ones, are hard to come by. One reason for this is that due to increased state requirements, schools and their teachers find themselves with less flexibility. This has caused teachers to be more scripted, leaving little room for innovative best practices to be developed and used successfully. Many schools also have a difficult time implementing best practices that have been successful in other schools. When this happens, it's an indication that the school is not set up to handle innovative teaching strategies aimed at twenty-first century learning. It often means that the education delivery system at that school is still stuck in the twentieth century.

That's where DSEI comes in. DSEI is the twenty-first century system that provides fertile ground for best practices to take root. When used within DSEI, best practices become powerful tools for student achievement and student improvement.

We've tapped our vast network of current and former teachers, administrators, principals, superintendents, and education consultants to find and collect field-tested and proven best practices.

We remain committed to building our collection of best practices. They evolve. We discover new ones as circumstances continue to change. And no doubt, as more schools join the effort to move our entire education system into the twenty-first century, you might even find yourself creating a new best practice. I invite you to share any with us at the International Center so that we can share them with more districts, schools, and teachers hungry to move their classrooms and schools forward.

Best Practices: DSEI Alignment Reference Charts

Each best practice is primarily aligned to one DSEI element from one of the three DSEI segments—organizational leadership, instructional leadership, and teaching. In several cases, multiple elements are aligned to a best practice in a secondary or tertiary capacity. The following chart will help you reference all of the best practices included in this section and the elements each one serves.

Best Practice	DSEI Alignment		
	Primary	Secondary	Tertiary
1. Why Not Us? (p. 116)	OL #1: Culture		
2. Attaining Excellent Achievement Through Strong School Culture (p. 118)	OL #1: Culture	OL #4: Leadership Capacity	OL #2: Vision
3. Creating a Vision Where Teachers and Staff Lead by Example (p. 122)	OL #2: Vision	OL #1: Culture	
4. Fiscal Responsibility to Student Achievement (p. 124)	OL #2: Vision	OL #1: Culture	
5. Twenty-First Century Learning Spaces (p. 126)	OL #3: Organizational Structure/ Systems	T #2: How Students Learn/Learner Engagement	
6. 3-D "Virtual Classrooms" (p. 128)	OL #3: Organizational Structure/ Systems	T #4: Instructional Strategies/ Technology	T #2: How Students Learn/Learner Engagement
7. Empowering Teachers to Lead (p. 130)	OL #4: Leadership Capacity		
8. Aligning Evaluation with Teacher Support (p. 133)	OL #5: Select/ Support/ Evaluate	OL #1: Culture	
9. Districtwide Data Newsletter (p. 137)	OL #6: Data Systems		
OL = Organizational Leadership IL = Instructional Leadership T = Teaching			

Best Practice	DSEI Alignment		
	Primary	Secondary	Tertiary
1. Creating an Inspiring Vision and Culture of "No Excuses" Teamwork (p. 142)	IL #1: High Expectations		
2. Literacy for All, No Exceptions (p. 145)	IL #1: High Expectations	OL #2: Vision	OL #1: Culture
3. Teaching Digital Literacy and Citizenship Skills (p. 152)	IL #2: Curriculum to Standards	T #4: Instructional Strategies/ Technology	
4. The Independent OpenCourseWare Study (IOCS) Program (p. 155)	IL #2: Curriculum to Standards	T #4: Instructional Strategies/ Technology	
5. Making Student Thinking Visible— Reflective Writing Across Content (p. 160)	IL #3: Integrate Math/Literacy	T #4: Instructional Strategies/ Technology	
6. Assigning a Curriculum Integration Leader (p. 163)	IL #3: Integrate Math/Literacy		
7. Close Reading in the Secondary Classroom (p. 165)	IL #3: Integrate Math/Literacy	T #4: Instructional Strategies/ Technology	
8. Measuring Perceptions of Rigor, Relevance, Relationships, and Leadership in a School (p. 172)	IL #4: Data to Drive Instruction	OL #1: Culture	T #1: RRR for All
OL = Organizational Leadership IL = Instructional Leadership T = Teaching			

Best Practice	DSEI Alignment		
	Primary	Secondary	Tertiary
9. Student Literacy Growth Profile (p. 174)	IL #4: Data to Drive Instruction	IL #3: Integrate Math/Literacy	
10. Data-in-a-Day (p. 177)	IL #4: Data to Drive Instruction		
11. Worlds of Learning @ NMHS—Digital Badges in Professional Learning (p. 178)	IL #5: Focused Professional Development		
12. Principal Professional Learning Communities (p. 181)	IL #5: Focused Professional Development		
13. Focus on Digital Learning Environments (p. 183)	IL #5: Focused Professional Development	OL #3: Organizational Structure/ Systems	
14. Equity Through Family Engagement: The King Project (p. 185)	IL #6: Family and Community Engagement in Learning	IL #1: High Expectations	OL #1: Culture
OL = Organizational Leadership IL = Instructional Leadership T = Teaching			

Best Practice	DSEI Alignment		
	Primary	Secondary	Tertiary
1. Developing a Product or Service: From Concept to Reality (p. 190)	T #1: RRR for All		
2. Early Career Awareness: Linking Lessons to Career Skills (p. 192)	T #1: RRR for All	T #4: Instructional Strategies/ Technology	
3. Creating Real Job Opportunities in the School (p. 194)	T #1: RRR for All		
4. Who Do We and Don't We Know? (p. 196)	T #1: RRR for All	OL #2: Vision	OL #1: Culture
5. Building Relationships Through Culturally Responsive Activities (p. 198)	T #1: RRR for All	OL #2: Vision	OL #1: Culture
6. Flipped Classroom (p. 200)	T #2: How Students Learn/Learner Engagement		
7. Developing Content Knowledge with Graphs and Charts Across the Curriculum (p. 203)	T #3: Content	IL #3: Integrate Math/Literacy	
8. Leveraging Technology to Teach Self-Directed Learning Skills (p. 213)	T #4: Instructional Strategies/ Technology	T #3: Content	
OL = Organizational Leadership IL = Instructional Leadership T = Teaching			

Best Practice	DSEI Alignment		
	Primary	Secondary	Tertiary
9. Book Buddies (p. 216)	T #4: Instructional Strategies/ Technology	IL #3: Integrate Math/Literacy	
10. Game-Based Learning in the Classroom (p. 218)	T #4: Instructional Strategies/ Technology	OL #3: Organizational Structure/ Systems	
11. Technology Integration Through *Julius Caesar* (p. 220)	T #4: Instructional Strategies/ Technology	T #2: How Students Learn/Learner Engagement	T #1: RRR for All
12. Formative Assessment: The Exit Ticket (p. 222)	T #5: Assessments		
13. Electronic Portfolio of Student Work (p. 224)	T #5: Assessments		
14. Focused Differentiated Instruction (p. 227)	T #5: Assessments	T #6: Professional Learning	
15. Literacy Workshops to Improve Literacy Across Subjects (p. 232)	T #6: Professional Learning	IL #3: Integrate Math/Literacy	
OL = Organizational Leadership IL = Instructional Leadership T = Teaching			

Chapter Nine

Organizational Leadership
Best Practices

OL Best Practice 1: Why Not Us?

Primary DSEI Alignment: Organizational Leadership

Element: Create a culture of high academic expectations and positive relationships

Submitted By: Thomas Miller, Principal, Brooks-Quinn-Jones Elementary School, Nacogdoches, Texas

Summary: A plan to foster a high sense of self-worth in each student, as well as a sense of community and belonging

Context

The digital age, and its accompanying social transformations and expectations, is necessitating a fundamental shift in schools from their current bureaucratic form and structure reflecting the factory model of the twentieth century to schools that function as modern learning organizations. A true learning organization can create the conditions and capacities most conducive for leaders, teachers, and students to perform at high levels and meet the expectations of rigorous new learning standards.

Overview and Process

Thomas Miller became the principal at Brooks-Quinn-Jones (BQJ) Elementary School in Nacogdoches, Texas, during the 2014–15 school year. As a new principal, he wanted to develop an initiative with the staff, students, and community that would begin to build strong relationships and give a voice to the BQJ community. He looked to the game of football for inspiration.

Miller was impressed with the story of the 5-foot 11-inch Seattle Seahawks quarterback, Russell Wilson, who led his team to the 2014 NFL championship despite being doubted throughout his career. He asked his teammates to believe that the Super Bowl was within reach.

"I remember my dad asking me one time, and it's something that has always stuck with me, 'Why not you, Russ?'" Wilson has been quoted saying. "You know, why not me? Why not me in the Super Bowl? So in speaking to our football team earlier in the year, I said, 'Why not us? Why can't we be there?'" (http://www.nfl.com/news/story/0ap2000000321904/article/seahawks-russell-wilson-on-super-bowl-why-not-us)

Each morning, Miller meets with students from Pre-K through third grades in the gym for the morning chant. He starts off by saying "Why Not You?" Students respond with, "Why Not Me!" He then says, "I am...," and the students say, "BQJ!" Miller says, "Because I...," and the students say "CARE!"

In the hallway, there are commitment pages for all to sign—community leaders who visit the campus, parents, teachers, students and, of course, the principal. Each commitment page has its own statement at the top, and people sign the page that pertains to them:

The Community said: "BECAUSE I CARE!"
The Principal said: "WHY NOT YOU!"
The Student said: "WHY NOT ME!"
The Teacher said: "WHY NOT US!"
They All Said: "ALL MEANS ALL!"

To further enhance the ubiquitous sense of belonging and community, Miller had bags printed for students with the slogan *Why Not Me!* Each grade level's bag has its own unique color and style. He also realized that in order for the BQJ faculty to buy into this transformation, they needed to be given the opportunity to have a say in school matters, so he created a web page dedicated to giving his new staff a medium to voice ideas. The faculty was asked to provide one or two ideas to help improve campus collegiality (campus involvement). They were also asked to suggest the best approach to involve teachers, parents, and community members (community involvement). These actions have successfully shifted the school culture in a collaborative and goal-oriented direction.

OL Best Practice 2: Attaining Excellent Achievement Through Strong School Culture

Primary DSEI Alignment: Organizational Leadership

Element: Create a culture of high academic expectations and positive relationships

Secondary DSEI Alignment: Organizational Leadership

Element: Build leadership capacity through an empowerment model

Tertiary DSEI Alignment: Organizational Leadership

Element: Establish a shared vision and communicate it to all constituent groups

Submitted By: Beth Howell, Principal, Kathleen H. Wilbur Elementary School, Bear, Del.

Summary: Creating a positive, engaging, and inclusive school culture that inspires students—and staff—to develop strong characters and a belief in their ability to achieve anything through hard work

Context

Wilbur Elementary School is Delaware's largest elementary school with a diverse population of more than 1,100 students. Our school offers a variety of educational and support programs to meet the varied needs of our students. We believe in proactively handling situations and pride ourselves on a positive school climate.

We decided our vision would be to inspire both students and teachers to come to school each day and strive to do more, achieve more, and enjoy learning together. To realize this vision, we knew that we first had to develop a positive, engaging, and inclusive culture— and this took time. We spent three years implementing and tweaking a series of strategies to help us meet our goal of creating a positive culture where everyone was galvanized around a shared vision of inspiration and motivation toward growth and achievement. A selection of those strategies follow.

Overview and Process

A Focus on Building Character

   Encouraging a Growth Mindset. According to the findings of psychologist Carol Dweck, detailed at length in her book *Mindset: The New Psychology of Success*, students with a fixed mindset believe that they have a certain amount of intelligence and there is not much that can be done to change it. Students with a growth mindset believe that with enough tenacity or "grit," they can achieve anything if they work hard enough. Test results have shown that students with a growth mindset continuously improve, where those with a fixed mindset generally do not. We decided that instilling in each of our students a growth mindset would become an overarching and schoolwide strategy. Whenever and wherever possible, we encouraged teachers to incorporate and emphasize this point.

   As part of our objective to raise expectations for all students, we teach students in all grades the difference between a growth mindset and a fixed mindset and how to recognize each, particularly as they pertain to learning. Students at Wilbur are taught to adjust thinking and self-talk so that they can combat the idea that they "can't" learn something. They know that their brains are constantly growing and that they have the power to learn through mistakes and perseverance. Through a commitment to this growth mindset initiative, teachers are regularly reinforcing with students how much they believe in them, and this has created a noticeable difference in students' own belief in themselves and their ability to improve.

   iCommunity. Another key initiative in creating a positive culture to realize our vision was what we call iCommunity, which is short for "inspiring community." iCommunity meetings are monthly school assemblies, each structured around a positive character trait such as perseverance, honesty, leadership, or a proactive response to negative thought.

   iCommunity meetings have a pep rally-like atmosphere. Students enter and exit to drum line music and do the Wilbur school cheer: "We are WILBUR. We are INSPIRED. Hard WORKERS. Great THINKERS. We PERSEVERE!" Using technology, videos, cooperative learning activities, and high-energy songs, all students participate in dialogues about scenarios that are related to the character trait theme. Following each iCommunity is a grade-level assembly where the character trait of the month is explained to the students in an age-appropriate manner.

To reinforce each tenet of character, we developed the idea of using five minutes of school lunchtime every day for what we call "Give Me 5." In the Give Me 5 activity, we set a positive tone for all students by covering a topic related to the month's character trait. These short activities include discussions about various situations, scenarios, and quotes, all of which are focused on peer interactions, improving group cohesiveness, and the appreciation of individual differences. These five minutes have become widely viewed as focused, fun, and an important time of the day that students and faculty alike look forward to.

These innovative character initiatives have been able to change the culture of our building radically. By placing a high standard on character traits and making them a priority throughout the entire school year, we are helping our students form positive visions of the people they want to become. Using forty minutes of every month for a character pep rally could be seen as wasting academic time. Instead, we see this time as an absolutely necessary investment in our students' well-being at school as well as their futures; our goal is for this time to issue positive returns over the course of each student's lifetime.

Continual Growth for Staff
Wilbur's focus on creating a positive working and continual growth environment for staff led to the use of regular, targeted professional development that balances high expectations with fun.

Dream Teams. Because the Response to Intervention initiative was being implemented in our district, we needed to come up with a way to provide constant, targeted professional development around reading and math intervention best practices. To ensure that no one was overwhelmed, each staff member was invited to be a part of a "dream team" that met twice a month.

We divide staff into three dream teams, each based on rigor, relevance, or relationships. Every other week, teacher leaders present a strategy based on their team's area of focus that can be used right away in the classroom. Teachers are then expected to take what they have learned back to their professional learning communities. Ultimately, the idea of dream teams is to equip teachers with an inventory of best practices to improve student achievement that they can implement easily and immediately. Best practices have included Kagan Structures (simple, step-by-step instructional strategies designed to increase student engagement and cooperation), relevant technology tools, positive discipline strategies, and project-based learning strategies.

Friday Game Day. Every other Friday, the school hosts a Friday Game Day where teachers partake in a carnival game. The game rotates each time, but each affords the opportunity for staff to earn "Beth Bucks," which can later be spent on instructional materials, casual dress passes, or late passes. This fun activity allows the staff to end their week on a positive note, while also serving as a light-hearted reminder of the growth mindset and high expectations for teaching and learning.

Wilbur has become a place where each and every student—as well as every teacher and staff member—obtains a growth mindset and can expect to find success. Community members and families are often reporting that Wilbur students are well-mannered, and they attribute this directly to the character building activities we do with them on a regular basis. Furthermore, these positive traits and behaviors follow and benefit students as they progress through their education experience in upper grades. When compared to other schools within our school district, the data shows that by the time our students reach the eighth grade, they outperform all other students in other feeder patterns on the state test.

OL Best Practice 3: Creating a Vision Where Teachers and Staff Lead by Example

Primary DSEI Alignment: Organizational Leadership

Element: Establish a shared vision and communicate it to all constituent groups

Secondary DSEI Alignment: Organizational Leadership

Element: Create a culture of high academic expectations and positive relationships

Submitted By: Matthew E. Calderón, Superintendent, Pembroke Central School District, Corfu, N.Y.

Summary: To teach students interpersonal skills, teachers must first learn and embody these skills themselves.

Context

Pembroke Central Schools are academically successful, a leader in the region. In May 2012, the district surveyed parents and community members to identify areas of focus that would help guide the new three-year plan. Academics were the highest priority, and the issues of character development and bullying prevention tied for second.

The roadmap for what the district needed to do academically was predetermined by the state and on solid footing. So the district staff devoted their attention to developing students' personal and relational skills, with a long-term focus on preparing students for successful collaboration in work environments. Despite a unified investment in these priorities, the district lacked a shared vision for how to approach instruction.

Overview and Process

A District Shared Decision-Making Committee was established to focus on how to best promote a "Safe and Supportive Learning Environment" (SSLE). The SSLE Committee reviewed current practices and investigated various program options for character education, bullying prevention, and student leadership development. After thorough deliberation, the district opted to implement The Leader in Me process, which is based on *The 7 Habits of Highly Effective People* by Stephen Covey.

As the committee began learning about the 7 Habits, it became apparent that they needed to integrate and apply them into their own lives before it would be possible to instill them into the students' hearts and minds. Since this determination was made, the committee has completed the following:

- Submitted follow-up plans to the regional BOCES to make 7 Habits professional development eligible for state aid; otherwise, it would not have been financially possible.
- Recruited 40 people—district faculty and staff, students, and members of community partner organizations—to volunteer three days of their time over the summer to receive the initial 7 Habits Signature Training.
- In the fall, six district employees—a special education teacher, two school counselors, a math teacher, the superintendent, and a bus driver—were trained to be in-house trainers of the 7 Habits. The goal is to have at least one trainer in each building.
- Over winter break, the in-house trainers facilitated the district's first 7 Habits Signature Training to faculty and staff who, once again, volunteered their time.
- Additional volunteer in-house trainings were slated to occur over February recess and spring break, continuing once again in the summer. Ultimately, the district's vision is to have every employee in the district receive the training.

If the adults in the community are able to develop their own personal skills, then they will be qualified to do the same for the students. The Leader in Me model has driven the vision and become part of the district and community culture, which is the necessary first step for success.

OL Best Practice 4: Fiscal Responsibility
to Student Achievement

Primary DSEI Alignment: Organizational Leadership

Element: Establish a shared vision and communicate it to all constituent groups

Secondary DSEI Alignment: Organizational Leadership

Element: Create a culture of high academic expectations and positive relationships

Submitted By: Dr. Ed Croom, Superintendent, Johnston County Schools, Smithfield, N.C.

Summary: A culture-driven policy to ensure that every last expenditure is likely to improve student achievement

Context
Educators have, and forever will, mention improving student performance as a top priority. However, when it comes to budgetary matters and fund allocations, student performance too often takes a back seat.

Like Bill Daggett, I always say, "Culture trumps strategy." Successful schools create a culture that supports improvement before they attempt to implement change. As the Superintendent of Johnston County Schools in North Carolina, I decided that we needed to create a culture that caused every employee in the district to consider how every action they made would impact student achievement.

Overview and Process
We put a new budgeting practice in place for all employees that work in Johnston County Schools. Every budgetary item that was proposed—no matter how small or seemingly insignificant—needed justification about how that expenditure would likely impact student performance.

To enact this process, I made the review of budgets and expenditures the responsibility of the Assistant Superintendent of Instruction. We believed that an experienced educator would be most qualified to determine how money spent would affect the students. If the proposed cost seemed that it would positively impact the students, it would then be passed along to the Assistant Superintendent of Finance.

OL Best Practice 5: Twenty-First Century Learning Spaces

Primary DSEI Alignment: Organizational Leadership

Element: Align organizational structures and systems to the vision

Secondary DSEI Alignment: Teaching

Element: Create and implement an effective learner environment that is engaging and aligned to learner needs

Submitted By: Dr. Luvelle Brown, Superintendent, Ithaca City School District, Ithaca, N.Y.

Summary: Reshaping the school environment to support and enable innovative instruction that puts the student at the center of active learning

Context

In all organizational systems, priorities change over time, but the structures that have been set in place often do not. As a result, we lose sight of how and why we do things the way we do. The more time that passes, the more those systems and structures—the form—dictate, drive, and define the organization's practices and behaviors—the function—instead of supporting and enabling them.

In schools, as in other organizations, form should follow function. As the fundamental culture and function of a school evolves, the physical form of the school must be redesigned to adapt. In the Ithaca City School District (ICSD) in New York, staff used learning science research to adapt and apply a concept and design for twenty-first century learning spaces for school classrooms, meetings spaces, and other education environments.

Overview and Process

In the 2013–14 school year, DeWitt Middle School in the ICSD began integrating pedagogic principles throughout the building to create unique learning environments that use every bit of space as a learning tool. The district refers to them as "ThinkSpaces," which are data-driven designs engineered specifically to support learning, alter teaching practices and strategies, and increase student engagement and achievement. They were conceived out of the Cornell-based Cabrera Research Lab. Its founders, Drs. Derek and Laura Cabrera, applied insights from cognitive science, human ecology, and physiology—considered major areas of learning science—to devise the ThinkSpace strategy and tools.

ThinkSpaces are model classrooms that incorporate writable desktops and wall space, hands-on and eyes-on learning tools, buoy chairs, scaffolding knowledge charts, and other innovative tools not found in many traditional schools. There is no teacher's desk at the front of the class and students are encouraged to move around the classroom to collaborate with other students on tasks.

The act of movement heightens student engagement and alertness. Students literally become active players in the learning environment, which is an empowering and exciting shift away from the passivity of sitting at a desk for an hour. All aspects of a ThinkSpace encourage activity.

On several days during the school year, ICSD teachers work intensively within the ThinkSpace to further grasp the form of these learning environments and the pedagogical practices they can use to support high levels of student engagement. In turn, the days teachers use to acclimate to the ThinkSpace experience increases their comfort and confidence with the art of teaching and the ability to use physical space as a tool for student empowerment in their learning process.

Interview and observational data has indicated higher levels of engagement without needing extensive differentiation. In addition, the form of the learning spaces facilitates integration of the expansive Common Core curriculum. An unanticipated outcome of the initiative has been a dramatic decrease in disruptive student behavior, which has virtually eliminated the need for behavioral intervention in schools with ThinkSpace.

OL Best Practice 6: 3-D "Virtual Classrooms"

Primary DSEI Alignment: Organizational Leadership

Element: Align organizational structures and systems to the vision

Secondary DSEI Alignment: Teaching

Element: Plan and provide learning experiences using effective research-based strategies that are embedded with best practices including the use of technology

Tertiary DSEI Alignment: Teaching

Element: Create and implement an effective learner environment that is engaging and aligned to learner needs

Submitted By: Eric Sheninger, Former Principal, New Milford High School, N.J.

Summary: Using technology to move the physical classroom into a virtual classroom, where teachers can easily monitor and assist students as they "meet" with peers in other classrooms to work collaboratively in learning and teaching each other concepts

Context
3-D virtual learning breaks down the barriers of the traditional classroom by allowing students to visit and communicate with students and instructors in other classrooms in the school and, possibly, around the world.

Overview and Process
New Milford High School in New Jersey is a high-tech school that offers students the unique experience of learning chemistry in a completely virtual setting. Equipped with a headset and a computer, students are able to communicate with other students throughout the school. Each student creates an avatar in his or her own likeness as part of the learning experience. The students then direct their avatars

to visit various "classrooms" on the computer and interact with others accordingly in those virtual 3-D environments.

In the virtual classrooms are whiteboards, or media boards, on which students can post almost anything they want, such as questions or YouTube videos to help each other understand chemistry concepts. This style of learning engages all students in some manner and allows instructors to monitor and assist each student individually far more easily than in a traditional classroom lecture setting.

The virtual learning concept is in step with how students communicate naturally with each other, so the enthusiasm displayed is higher than expected.

Although the virtual chemistry classroom is a pilot program, teachers at New Milford expect the technology to be schoolwide in the near future and available on a broader range of mobile devices. Eventually, students will have access to virtual learning technology at home and will be able to communicate and interact with their teachers, school peers, and someday, possibly even students from around the world.

OL Best Practice 7: Empowering Teachers to Lead

Primary DSEI Alignment: Organizational Leadership

Element: Build leadership capacity through an empowerment model

Submitted By: Marilyn Boerke, Principal, Liberty Middle School, Camas, Wash.

Summary: A district-led teacher–leader program is a powerful way to empower teachers, boost morale, and free up time for organizational and instructional leadership to address higher level or more urgent matters.

Context
Public school districts face a number of challenges: increased demands and responsibilities on administrators, new standards and assessments and their impact on teaching and learning, and high teacher and principal turnover rates, to name just a few. Many organizational leaders are realizing that they have to delegate to stay afloat and not lose sight of the big picture; and they are realizing the same for their instructional leaders. Seeing an opportunity not only to delegate, but also to empower teachers, more and more districts are tapping effective teachers to take on more active leadership roles in both policy and practice as part of a full-scale teacher-leader initiative.

Overview and Process
The idea of teachers taking on leadership roles is not new, but the announcement of the Teach-to-Lead Initiative by the U.S. Department of Education and the National Board for Professional Teaching Standards created a groundswell of momentum for the concept. Camas School District in Washington State has developed and implemented a teacher–leadership empowerment model that leans on its most effective teachers to help plan for and share in the vast workload responsibilities of organizational and instructional leadership.

In Camas, district administrators worked with instructional leadership to identify the most effective teachers who demonstrated either an interest in or an ability to take on leadership roles, and then assigned them projects based on their expertise. Under the guidance of district leaders, these teachers then led their peers through new initiatives, like rolling out major policy initiatives. One teacher took the lead in creating a professional development program for all teaching staff around effective implementation of the new standards. Another teacher led an initiative to draft the district's template for writing and measuring student-growth goals, which are required under Washington's teacher evaluation system.

Central administration is becoming increasingly aware that they cannot merely give orders and expect smooth, enthusiastic implementation. And both the central office and school principals are becoming increasingly aware that principals alone cannot run a building. Rapid improvement comes only when leadership is encouraged at every level. Districts that launch teacher–leader programs and collaborate with principals to delegate responsibilities to teachers in a thoughtful way have experienced amazing turnaround. The inclusive decision-making process not only improves morale, but teacher–leaders also feel more confident and the school at large becomes infused with a renewed energy to get things done.

In creating a teacher–leadership team, it is critical to identify and select the most qualified and appropriate individuals to serve. These teacher–leaders must have the respect of the other staff as well as possess the qualities that fit the vision and needs of the school and district. Once in place, they will have the ability to effect change that the district leaders or principal cannot by virtue of being removed from other faculty or simply do not have time to do. Thus, important initiatives, like professional development or teaching training, don't have to fall by the wayside due to overload on leadership. Furthermore, by delegating certain tasks, district leaders and principals will find some of their time freed up for their more important and vision-driven responsibilities, like observing what is happening in the classrooms and guiding teachers through more student-oriented instruction.

On a schoolwide and districtwide level, the implementation of a teacher–leader program, and the culture of empowerment and inclusiveness that comes with it, makes a noticeable and positive impact on culture felt by all stakeholders.

Reference

Superville, Denisa R. (2015). "School districts turn to teachers to lead." *Education Week*, January 21, 2015. http://www.edweek.org/ew/articles/2015/01/21/school-districts-turn-to-teachers-to-lead.html

OL Best Practice 8: Aligning Evaluation with Teacher Support

Primary DSEI Alignment: Organizational Leadership

Element: Align teacher/leader selection, support, and evaluation

Secondary DSEI Alignment: Organizational Leadership

Element: Create a culture of high academic expectations and positive relationships

Submitted By: Scott Traub, Executive Director, West Region, International Center for Leadership in Education

Summary: The Collaborative Instructional Review Process is a strategic process to equip organizational and instructional leadership to implement an ongoing, collaborative, and positive teacher development program to support a culture of high expectations for all.

Context

Yakima School District (YSD) in Yakima, Wash., sought to create a districtwide culture of high expectations with a support system to help everyone meet those high expectations. To achieve this, they knew leader and teacher development and ongoing support was imperative. A system of just evaluation and remediation was not an option, as such practices tend to demoralize and create a culture of fear. Instead, district leaders set out to build a total talent management system; the goal was to hire leaders and teachers who demonstrate a cultural fit, and then provide ongoing professional development support to help everyone perform to his or her highest potential. A second aim of the professional development program was to make everyone in the district feel supported in not only meeting high expectations around education delivery, but also their personal professional goals. YSD leaders recognized that when leaders and teachers are meeting personal and instructional goals, then entire schools and districts can meet student achievement goals.

As part of the larger talent management system, YSD leaders were looking for a tool that would help instructional leaders support each of their building teachers toward consistent improvement. The district decided to use the International Center for Leadership in Education's (ICLE) proprietary Collaborative Instructional Review Process (CIR). CIR is a process that brings principals and teachers together to determine the prevalence of rigor, relevance, and learner engagement in instruction. It is not a performance evaluation tool, but rather a way to understand where instruction needs to be more rigorous and relevant and where learner engagement needs to be enhanced. In turn, it becomes a process for teacher improvement, while also serving to increase communication between school leadership and teachers. To help ensure optimized CIR implementation and sustained, successful use, the district enlisted the help of International Center coaches; each school leadership team worked with a coach to incorporate the process into their schools.

Overview and Process

CIR is a twofold process: the first component is training and equipping the leadership team with tools to become impactful instructional leaders and coaches to teachers. The leadership team engaged in training which entailed:

- Establishing and communicating clear expectations around student learning, instructional excellence, and effective practices.
- Defining a common voice and shared vocabulary for rigorous, relevant, and engaging instruction.
- Supporting every teacher in continuously improving instruction through targeted feedback, reflective practice, and ongoing application.
- Aligning CIR rubrics with Charlotte Danielson's Framework for Teaching—used statewide—to create the Yakima Instructional Framework.
- Creating a collaborative relationship in which teachers feel supported rather than evaluated.
- Embracing a formative process through which teachers receive ongoing feedback throughout the year.

Once this groundwork was set, the next objective of supporting teachers, providing ongoing feedback, and collaborating with them in setting and achieving improvement goals began. This includes a four-step process:

- **Step 1: Pre-visit.** Using a pre-observation form submitted by each teacher, the instructional leader facilitates a collaborative conversation to build understanding, clarify expectations, establish focus, and review the rubrics that will be used during the classroom lesson. The leader and teacher then digests and reflects on the conversation in advance of the classroom visit.
- **Step 2: Visit.** The leader then visits each classroom, spending about 80 percent of the time observing students, and the remaining 20 percent observing teachers. Using CIR's indicators of effective rigorous and relevant instruction as an observation rubric, the instructional leader collects evidence of student learning and takes notes for the debrief discussion.
- **Step 3: Debrief.** Through a collaborative discussion about the rubric and supporting evidence from the observation, instructional leaders support the teacher in action planning and applying feedback on instructional strategies to increase rigor, relevance, and engagement.
- **Step 4: Apply.** The teacher applies the feedback and action plan to instruction.

Changing a school's culture does not happen overnight; it is a long, complicated process that requires a clearly set objective and clearly articulated plan to get everyone there.

Our team of ICLE coaches guided YSD's leadership team through the process of CIR. As a result, all school leaders were equipped with the tools to implement in their schools a collaborative teacher support program.

From there, we took what we learned in the district sessions to individual school leadership teams. School leaders were encouraged by organizational leadership to adapt initiatives to their own school's DNA. School leadership teams assembled strategic planning sessions.

In addition to the assistance from ICLE's coaches, this laid the foundation for how to effectively position and consistently implement a collaborative approach to creating a culture of a positive, sustained, and impactful teacher support system.

We were then ready to begin the collaborative support process in each school. An ICLE coach accompanied each leader on three classroom observation visits, during which both the coach and leader took notes on their observations. Per CIR, the aim is primarily to observe students' apparent level of engagement, and secondarily to observe the teacher—although both are equally important. After the visits, the coach and leader compared their support evidence and rubric ratings and the coach provided additional considerations for future class visits. Once leaders calibrated their ratings, the leader was prepared to conduct independent observations, facilitate debrief sessions, and work with each teacher to devise an action plan to apply feedback.

CIR has become a fixture at YSD. Through its process, they collaborate frequently and regularly with teachers to ensure they have the support they need and work with them as they continue to raise the expectation on instruction—and, as a byproduct—on student achievement. Their success story in creating an effective and engaging learning environment, not just for students, but also for teachers, is just one of many in the district.

OL Best Practice 9: Districtwide Data Newsletter

Primary DSEI Alignment: Organizational Leadership

Element: Support decision making with relevant data systems

Submitted By: James Bruni, Director of Curriculum & Technology, Seneca Falls Central School District, Seneca Falls, N.Y.

Summary: Compiling a regular, districtwide newsletter detailing recent data and analyses to update everyone in the district on student achievement and goal progression and inform instructional needs

Context
Relevant, easy-to-use data systems are a highly effective tool that organizational leaders can use to support decision making and disseminate information to educators throughout the district. Meaningful data systems are the key to monitoring student improvement and progress toward goals as well as informing instruction. When data is used effectively at all levels of the education system, it provides opportunities for substantive conversations about student knowledge and achievement, teacher growth, and goal attainment.

Overview and Process
At Seneca Falls Central School District in New York (SFCSD), district leadership realized that an effective and efficient way to provide informative data on all students would be in the form of a periodic, districtwide data newsletter that promotes a K–12 approach to data and assessments.

The newsletter is a non-intimidating medium that all K–12 teachers can access to become aware of the data indicators and assessments being tracked in the district. The newsletter serves as a benchmark reminder to faculty that what they do every day is important and has vertical implications throughout the school system.

The response to the newsletter has been very positive among all district educators. It has been found to be a productive vehicle for generating informed, open, and data-driven discussions.

A key component to creating an effective, easy-to-read newsletter is high-quality graphics with minimal narrative. Visually appealing and diverse representations of data are more accessible than data that is either written about or presented as all numbers in a table.

The organization of the data—i.e., the order in which information is presented—is important. Begin first with indicators that inform who the students are, not how they do academically. Student enrollment and demographic data provide revealing insights into the students and, to an extent, the community as a whole. Trends in enrollment of various at-risk students or those enrolled in specific programs highlight unique challenges or successes occurring in the district. (See Figure 1.)

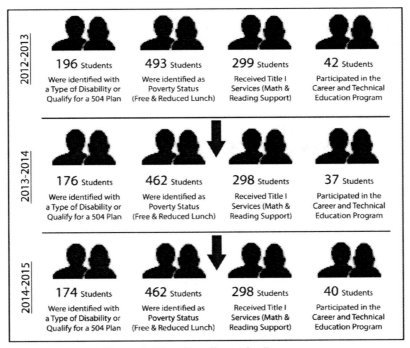

Figure 1. Class Enrollment by Program

The next section of the newsletter should highlight areas where the district is doing well or improving. For example, increased graduation and post-secondary rates, higher attendance, new AP or virtual courses offered, district performance compared to other local education agencies, etc. (See Figure 2.)

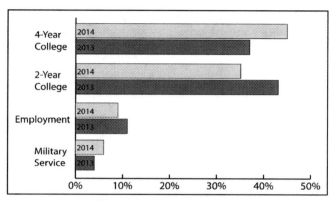

Figure 2. Graduation Data

The subsequent section of the newsletter begins to drill deeper into student performance. Both longitudinal (cohort-based) and cross-sectional (grade-to-grade; year-to-year) analyses can be used. An example of a longitudinal analysis would be to show growth in percent of students in the Class of 2014 at proficient or higher levels on state assessments from grade 8 to grade 11. A cross-sectional analysis shines more light on certain grades where student performance dips, especially if the lower performance is evident over multiple years. (See Figure 3.)

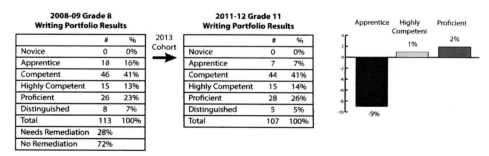

Figure 3. Writing Portfolio Results by Cohort

The final section of the newsletter should highlight nontraditional programs and/or nonmandated assessments that the district uses to measure student math or reading literacy levels. SFCSD assesses students at the elementary and intermediate grade levels to determine reading levels. The Developmental Reading Assessment (DRA) is used to monitor instructional reading levels and the Qualitative Reading Inventory (QRI) measures reading levels and comprehension. (See Figure 4.)

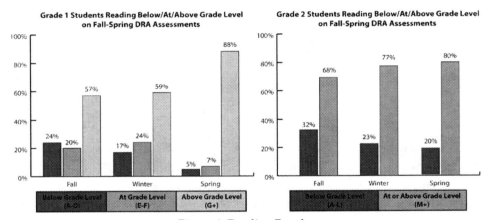

Figure 4. Reading Results

SFCSD uses STAR reading and math assessments to screen students' benchmark levels for possible intervention. Furthermore, the STAR assessment for reading has the ability to provide student Lexile measures, which can be used to match the reader to books suitable to his or her literacy level. SFCSD uses Lexile text measures to monitor the appropriateness of instructional texts at each grade and to show the necessary progression of the complexity of texts over time for college and career readiness.

Chapter Ten

Instructional Leadership
Best Practices

IL Best Practice 1: Creating an Inspiring Vision and Culture of "No Excuses" Teamwork

Primary DSEI Alignment: Instructional Leadership

Element: Use research and establish the urgent need for change to promote higher academic expectations and positive relationships

Submitted By: Rob Carroll, Principal, South Heights Elementary School, Henderson, Ky.

Summary: Creating a culture of regular goal-setting supported by an execution process that keeps all goals and their progress top of mind and enhances a sense of schoolwide duty and responsibility to all

Context

All constituents in our extended school community (students, staff, parents, community partners, and groups of alumni) gather on a regular basis to refine the vision for our school. Together we create goals—outside of local, state, and national mandates—that define our culture and drive the efforts and initiatives of our school. We commit to achieving each new round of goals within five years. The excitement and call to action generated by the momentum to meet these goals is highly motivating and continually propels us forward. Everyone understands that this is a team effort, which fosters a sense of duty to each other and creates a culture where there is no room for excuses.

Overview and Process

We are constantly refreshing and refining our goals and creating new ones, always with the aim of maintaining high expectations and building a clear schoolwide plan to get us all to meet those expectations. An overview of strategies and tactics we've employed to support our vision for a "no excuses" culture follows.

- **Making goals known and top of mind**. Each time we create a new list of objectives for a five-year timeframe, we list all goals on large vision boards. They are then displayed in the main school hallway. A countdown clock runs continuously next to each vision board until its five-year period expires. The idea is for everyone in the school to regularly and frequently pass by these boards so that goals stay top of mind. We put checkmarks next to goals as they are achieved. On a daily basis, students are involved in goal tracking attainment by monitoring timelines and "check-offs" on the vision boards. Monitoring progress is a daily activity and a key step in our school improvement process.

- **Encouraging teamwork and cultivating leadership in everyone**. With all eyes on our goals in a routine way, we cultivate interdependence between and a sense of responsibility in everyone in the extended school community. Everyone understands that the success of the whole group is dependent on each individual. This naturally encourages leadership in every last student; each student must take the lead in playing his or her part in advancing the entire school toward goals.

- **Frequent use of data to show progress and recalibrate strategies as needed**. We determined that combining traditional student data (test scores, pre- and post-assessments) with non-traditional data (surveys, student polls) would help us monitor the strength of the school's culture. We use data to guide our improvement efforts for everything from school culture to leadership improvement plans. Even the principal's performance is included in the assessments; team members evaluate the principal each month through anonymous feedback forms. Using these different quantitative and qualitative data sets provides us with ongoing snapshots of where we are as a school relative to our objectives. It also informs where and how we need to recalibrate or improve our strategies to ensure we meet all goals.

- **Interdisciplinary instruction**. One of our larger goals was to make all learning interdisciplinary. To that end, we developed content teams, which regularly meet to share in the planning and implementation of agreed-upon strategies that align interdisciplinary instruction across the curriculum and between grades for individual subject areas.

The school has applied a rigorous, clear plan for improving its culture. The most notable reflections of our efforts and team commitment to improvement are the reduced number of discipline referrals, increased attendance rates, and better achievement on state assessments.

IL Best Practice 2: Literacy for All, No Exceptions

Primary DSEI Alignment: Instructional Leadership

Element: Use research and establish the urgent need for change to promote higher academic expectations and positive relationships

Secondary DSEI Alignment: Organizational Leadership

Element: Establish a shared vision and communicate it to all constituent groups

Tertiary DSEI Alignment: Organizational Leadership

Element: Create a culture of high academic expectations and positive relationships

Submitted By: Dr. Susan Szachowicz, Principal (Retired), Brockton High School, Brockton, Mass.; adapted from *Transforming Brockton High School*

Summary: A systematic process to change the collective staff mindset to one of a shared responsibility for every last student's literacy achievement, supported by raised expectations for all

Context

In 1998, the Commonwealth of Massachusetts instituted its high-stakes testing program in English and math, the MCAS. In response, an administrator at Brockton High School stood before the faculty and declared that the tests were much too hard for Brockton students and that most students would surely never earn a diploma. Given the "right to fail" attitude prevalent in the school, not surprisingly the initial MCAS scores placed Brockton as one of the lowest-performing schools in the state. The school was mired in low expectations, excuse-making, and a leadership that was unwilling to look inward for ways to improve.

Overview and Process

The genesis of Brockton High's turnaround began with a team of faculty and administrators whose main motivation was to tackle the MCAS performance problem. Initial attempts to recruit team members were not easy: many faculty did not want to be bothered. A more aggressive and persistent recruitment of faculty members that were viewed as leaders was more fruitful. In all, 22 members were assembled to form the Restructuring Committee.

The Restructuring Committee dissected the MCAS from every angle in an attempt to understand what skills and competencies every student would need to obtain proficiency. Developing this list was fairly straightforward. What proved more difficult, and led to many concerned observations, was evaluating our own practices regarding the rigor of our standards and the quality and consistency of instruction across the school. Ultimately, the Committee was faced with the question, "Is this the best we can be?" As it turned out, the answer was a resounding, "NO!"

This powerful admission allowed us finally to have honest conversations around how we were failing our students. From this came the game-changing epiphany: we were failing to teach them literacy. This sparked our schoolwide focus on literacy and its four components: reading, writing, speaking, and reasoning. These became the core values that anchored the discussions and planning in the committee's meetings from that point forward. For students to be successful, each teacher in every department needed to buy in to this shift in mindset around literacy instruction.

A common definition of literacy needed to be developed. The group divided into four subcommittees as an attempt to articulate the specific skills and competencies that students needed to master in the four literacy areas. The lists of skills and competencies had to adhere to the following criteria and be:

- Clearly stated so that anyone—student, parent, teacher, community member—would understand the skill
- Interdisciplinary—applicable in every class and subject
- Applicable for all students—from gifted and talented to those most in need

The committee created four charts, collectively referred to as the literacy charts, to provide visual representation of skills and competencies. The charts listed the corresponding skills for each of the four components of literacy: reading, writing, speaking, and reasoning.

Our next challenge was to present the literacy initiative to the other faculty and administration at Brockton High, which totaled more than 300 individuals. Aware that the literacy initiative would likely be met with tremendous resistance, the committee knew they had to communicate emphatically to faculty that they would have a strong voice in the initiative's development and implementation.

The committee was allotted 45 minutes of work time for each semi-monthly meeting with faculty; a focused agenda was required. Keeping the faculty discussions interdisciplinary was a key decision in propelling the literacy initiative forward. Many faculty associated within their discipline only, and Brockton is so large that many teachers often don't know teachers in different departments. The Committee wanted to break down those content walls so that everyone could focus on literacy as a schoolwide initiative rather than as a subject-specific one.

The committee began by dividing the faculty into interdisciplinary discussion groups of 12–15 teachers. Each group was facilitated by a different committee member. Every teacher was provided with the drafts of the four literacy charts. At the top of the charts, we put the students' MCAS scores (41 percent failed English and 76 percent failed math) with this question, "Is this the BEST we can be?" The facilitators had the following outline for navigating their group discussion:

1. Explain why we are focusing on the MCAS, but also remind teachers that school improvement is about more than just test scores. It's about helping students improve their academic performance and preparing them for life after graduation.

2. Explain that the goal of the meeting is to review and revise the literacy charts. To do so, pose these questions:

   • In each of the four literacy areas, have we included what is required for our students to be successful in your class/your content area? If not, what skills or competencies are missing?

   • Is each literacy skill stated clearly so that all teachers and students can understand it? If not, how would you rephrase it?

   • Literacy is not only the domain of English classes. Students should be demonstrating these skills and applying them in every classroom with proficiency. Is each skill applicable to your content area? To all content areas? When you read the skills, do you find yourself saying, "Yes, a student should be able to do this in my class"? If not, how should we rephrase these skills? Should any be omitted?

In all, the drafts of the literacy charts were revised four or five times with the faculty before the committee settled on the final versions. The charts were then posted in every classroom in the school to serve as a constant reminder of both literacy's link to all subject areas and the school's vision for literacy for all. They represented a significant change in mindset at Brockton High. They defined the school's high academic expectations for student learning in specific, measurable ways and gave Brockton High a common focus for the first time. Reading, writing, speaking, and reasoning skills were no longer viewed as the responsibility of the English department; they were the shared responsibility of all teachers in all departments.

The final versions of the four literacy charts follow:

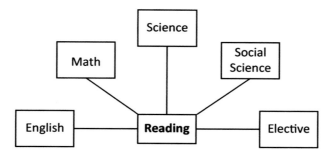

- for content (both literal and inferential)
- to apply pre-reading, during reading, and
  post-reading strategies to all reading assignments,
  including determining purpose and pre-learning vocabulary
- to research a topic
- to gather information
- to comprehend an argument
- to determine the main idea of a passage
- to understand a concept and construct meaning
- to expand one's experiences

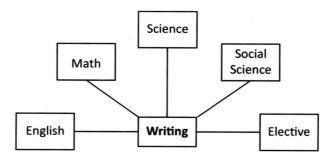

- to take notes
- to explain one's thinking
- to argue a thesis and support one's thinking
- to compare and contrast
- to write an open response
- to describe an experiment, report one's findings, and report
  one's conclusions
- to generate a response to what one has heard, viewed, or read
- to convey one's thinking in complete sentences
- to develop an expository essay with a formal structure

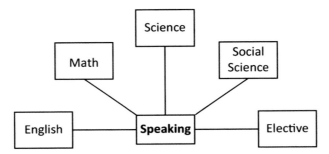

- to convey one's thinking in complete sentences
- to interpret a passage orally
- to debate an issue
- to participate in class discussion or a public forum
- to make an oral presentation to one's class, one's peers, one's community
- to present one's portfolio
- to respond to what one has read, viewed, or heard
- to communicate in a manner that allows one to be both heard and understood

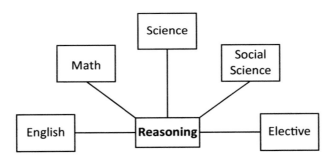

- to create, interpret, and explain a table, chart, or graph
- to compute, interpret, and explain numbers
- to read, break down, and solve a word problem
- to interpret and present statistics that support an argument or hypothesis
- to identify a pattern, explain a pattern, and/or make a prediction based on a pattern
- to detect the fallacy in an argument or a proof
- to explain the logic of an argument or solution
- to use analogies and/or evidence to support one's thinking
- to explain and/or interpret relationships of space and time

The dramatic, substantive changes at Brockton High have taken hard work, a tenacious focus on improving student academic achievement, and an unwillingness to give up on any student. Long gone are the days where administration predicted students would not pass the MCAS and lamented all the challenges and disadvantages that Brockton High faced. Today, Brockton High is proactively focused only on the academic success of every student, and faculty now eagerly await MCAS scores to celebrate student and teacher achievement.

IL Best Practice 3: Teaching Digital Literacy and Citizenship Skills

Primary DSEI Alignment: Instructional Leadership

Element: Develop, implement, and monitor standards-aligned curriculum and assessments

Secondary DSEI Alignment: Teaching

Element: Plan and provide learning experiences using effective research-based strategies that are embedded with best practices including the use of technology

Submitted By: Tammy Russell, Principal; Angela Robert, Director of Instruction; Danielle Chapman, Instruction Support; and Tim Davey, Technology Instructor, Salmon River Middle School, Fort Covington, N.Y.

Summary: Using tools to teach students how to understand the larger, long-term implications of Internet use, behave appropriately and sensitively online, and use technology responsibly and efficiently

Context

The immense power of digital media gives students extraordinary opportunities to explore, connect, create, and learn in ways never before imagined. A survey of more than 330 students in our rural middle school in far northern New York State revealed that 89 percent of our students access social media sites inside and outside of school. Although these powerful, socially interactive technologies have seemingly limitless potential, young people are vulnerable in ways unlike ever before. Meanwhile, schools are dealing with associated consequences, like cyberbullying, digital cheating, and safety and security concerns. These issues underscore the need for students to learn—and for teachers to teach—digital literacy and citizenship skills.

Overview and Process

At Salmon River Middle School, it became apparent that some action needed to be taken to educate students in responsible and safe technology use and its impact. In searching for a tool or initiative that was both financially equitable and programmatically effective, Common Sense Media's free Digital Literacy and Citizenship Curriculum was ultimately selected. (https://www.commonsensemedia.org/educators/curriculum)

The curriculum empowers students to think critically, behave safely, and participate responsibly in the digital world. Providing lessons with these twenty-first-century skills is essential for students to harness the full potential of technology for learning. The aim of the initiative is to enable students to make smart, responsible, respectful decisions when using digital media. At the same time, it is important that educators help students understand the ethical consequences behind the actions and decisions that they make online.

There are 80 lessons in the full K–12 Common Sense Media curriculum, with supporting materials such as student handouts, assessments, educational videos, family tip sheets, and professional development resources. Common Sense Media suggests starting with its Scope & Sequence to determine which approach is appropriate for the students. The Scope & Sequence consists of three units for grade bands K–2, 3–5, and 6–8 and four units for Grades 9–12. Each unit is comprised of five lessons, which spiral to address a cross-curricular approach. The units build on each other by reinforcing developmentally appropriate topics. Schools can use the units either sequentially by grade or at any grade level within this band.

Salmon River Middle School opted for the Scope & Sequence for grades 6–8. Each of the three units begins with a self-image and identity lesson, which is designed to help students explore their own digital lives, focusing on their online versus offline identity. Through lessons, students obtain information literacy skills to identify, find, evaluate, and use information effectively.

Students also learn strategies for managing their online information and keeping it secure through lessons about privacy and security. Learning about the digital footprint and online reputations shows students how to protect their own privacy and respect others' privacy. In various lessons within the units, students reflect on how they can use interpersonal skills to build and strengthen positive online communication and communities. Cyberbullying and Internet safety are addressed to teach strategies for handling cyberbullying and situations or online behavior that may make them uncomfortable. Students are given pre- and post-assessments to measure knowledge gained and skills acquired from each unit. (https://www.commonsensemedia.org/educators/scope-and-sequence)

IL Best Practice 4: The Independent OpenCourseWare Study (IOCS) Program

Primary DSEI Alignment: Instructional Leadership

Element: Develop, implement, and monitor standards-aligned curriculum and assessments

Secondary DSEI Alignment: Teaching

Element: Plan and provide learning experiences using effective research-based strategies that are embedded with best practices including the use of technology

Submitted By: Eric Sheninger, Former Principal, New Milford High School, N.J.

Summary: Using OpenCourseWare to provide students opportunities to create an individualized, interest- and passion-based learning experience derived from courses at top American universities.

Context

OpenCourseWare (OCW) is a free and open, web-based publication of high-quality educational materials, organized by courses from outstanding American universities. OCW courses are available under open licenses, such as Creative Commons.

The Independent OpenCourseWare Study (IOCS) Program was developed by Juliana Meehan and Eric Sheninger and pioneered at New Milford High School in New Milford, N.J. It represents a bold, authentic learning experience for secondary students that allows them to fully utilize OCW to pursue learning that focuses on their passions, interests, and career aspirations. IOCS is aligned to national standards, ISTE Standards, and state technology standards as well as P21's Skills Framework for 21st Century Learning.

IOCS students choose from an array of OpenCourseWare offerings from MIT, Harvard, Yale, UC Berkeley, Stanford, and many other universities and apply their learning to earn high school credit.

Overview and Process

Students choose an OCW course (or part of a course) from an approved, accredited university through the IOCS website. Using the IOCS Google Docs registration form embedded in the site, they register for their course by identifying the institution, course number, and title. Sometimes, if the course is extensive or very advanced, students may decide to complete only certain parts of the course, in which case they identify which part(s) they agree to complete at the outset. This is taken into account when their work is assessed.

Once they choose their OCW course, students engage in the activities assigned to that particular unit of study. Learning activities vary widely from institution to institution and within disciplines, but coursework usually consists of one or more of the following: course lectures, which can be video presentations or texts; learning activities, such as experiments or open-ended questions; demonstrations; and interim and final assessments. Students apply themselves to these activities over the duration of a high school marking period.

Students receive individualized mentoring as they progress through their OCW course. Highly motivated and gifted students who have found their "perfect" course may need little guidance, while others may benefit from varying degrees of structure and advice along the way. IOCS mentors check in with students on a regular basis to gauge the level of mentoring intervention needed. In all cases, the advanced content and high expectations inherent in the coursework provides students with a glimpse into the demands that college poses and helps them prepare for higher education.

Students combine their creativity with their newfound knowledge to synthesize a unique product that demonstrates and applies the new knowledge and skills they gained from the OCW. The aim is for students to go beyond a static PowerPoint presentation laden with mere text and pictures. Instead, the objective is for students to produce an actual product, whether it is the demonstration of a new skill, the creation of a physical model, the designing and conducting of an experiment, the formulation of a theory, or some other creative way to show what they've learned.

The culminating IOCS experience is a five- to seven-minute student exposition of learning in front of faculty and IOCS peers. The work is assessed according to the IOCS Rubric, as seen on pages 158–159, which is aligned to national and state standards. Student products are rated as Not Proficient, Proficient, or Outstanding for each of the following criteria: Physical Product, Technology, Depth of Learning, Public Speaking, and Studentship. The IOCS Rubric follows.

The IOCS Rubric

	Outstanding	Proficient	Not Proficient
Physical Product (5 points)	Student uses authentic tools and props to convey new knowledge acquired through specified OpenCourseWare from an approved institution of learning; this can include but is not limited to demonstration of a new skill, learning a new technology, creating a physical model, designing and conducting an experiment, and formulation of a theory.	Student uses some tools or props in addition to a demonstration of knowledge acquired through specified OpenCourseWare from an approved institution of learning in the form of a traditional presentation stemming from specified OpenCourseWare from an approved institution of learning.	Student has lectured on the subject of content from OpenCourseWare from an approved institution, but no physical project is presented other than a PowerPoint, PREZI, or other digital presentation tool that contains an abundance of text, but lacks depth.
Technology (5 points)	Student has creatively integrated 2 or more technological tools and/or media resources in the construction of his/her knowledge and development of the final product.	Student has creatively integrated 1 technological tool or media resource in the construction of his/her knowledge and development of the final product.	Student did not integrate any technological tool or media resource in the construction of his/her knowledge and development of the final product.
Depth of Learning (5 points)	Exposition of learning clearly demonstrates acquisition and application of new knowledge; student is able to answer audience questions and demonstrate extended knowledge; student is likely to be able to apply learning from this project to college and career goals.	Exposition of learning demonstrates some acquisition and application of new knowledge; student may be able to answer some additional questions from audience; student may be able to apply learning from this project to college and career goals.	Exposition does not demonstrate new knowledge. OR The student shows little understanding of the knowledge or skills involved and is unlikely to be able to apply learning from this project to college and career goals.

The IOCS Rubric (continued)

Public Speaking (5 points)	Student presented original goals as well as claims and findings; ideas were sequenced logically and with pertinent descriptions, facts and details to accentuate main ideas; a concise summarization was provided; there was appropriate eye contact, adequate volume and clear, correct pronunciation; student showed enthusiasm for this work.	Student presented original goals or claims and findings; ideas were presented with pertinent descriptions, facts and details to accentuate main ideas; a summarization was provided; student attempted to provide eye contact, adequate volume, and correct pronunciation; student showed enthusiasm for this work.	Presentation lacked one or more of the following: original goals, claims/findings; pertinent descriptions, facts, details, or summarization; appropriate eye contact, adequate volume, and clear, correct pronunciation. Student may not have shown enthusiasm for this work.
Studentship (5 points)	All IOCS directions were followed carefully and forms filled out; all goals outlined at the outset of the project were met and completed on time; presentation was kept within time limits; all forms and feedback requirements were met. All works cited and consulted were presented in correct MLA format.	IOCS directions were generally followed carefully and all forms filled out; some but not all goals were outlined at the outset of the project; specified goals were completed on time; presentation may have been kept within time limits; most or all forms and feedback requirements were met; sources cited and consulted were presented.	One or more of the following is evident: IOCS directions/forms not carefully followed/ filled out; goals were not outlined at the outset of the project and may not have been completed on time; presentation not kept within time limits; forms/ feedback requirements not met; works cited and consulted not presented.

TOTAL PROJECT SCORE: _____

*Grading key: A+ = 14-15 points; A=12-13; A-=11; B+=10; B=9; B-=8; C+=7.
Below 7 points requires redo of project.*

IL Best Practice 5: Making Student Thinking Visible— Reflective Writing Across Content

Primary DSEI Alignment: Instructional Leadership

Element: Integrate literacy, math, and technology across all disciplines

Secondary DSEI Alignment: Teaching

Element: Plan and provide learning experiences using effective research-based strategies that are embedded with best practices including the use of technology

Submitted by: Catherine Truitt and Diane Jones, Consultants, International Center for Leadership in Education

Summary: A reflective writing toolkit to move students away from merely reporting on what they've learned, and instead write critically and analytically about the larger context of their learning to promote literacy in all subjects

Context

Within the realm of new English language arts standards, the idea that presents the biggest change and challenge for schools is that literacy is now considered a shared responsibility. Reading and writing must be part of daily instruction for students in all subjects. Furthermore, the new, more rigorous standards require that students produce evidence-based writing across content as well as writing that informs and persuades.

Reflective writing is evidence of reflective thinking. Meaningful intellectual engagement comes when students make connections between ideas, which strengthens and reinforces critical and analytical thinking. Ultimately, this leads to new levels of understanding and higher retention of information.

Overview and Process

Rather than asking students to summarize information or report on facts, reflective writing allows them to write about their own learning in a rigorous and relevant way. Reflective writing—where critical and reflective thinking meet—encourages students to write about ways new learning fits into prior and existing knowledge.

The table of reflective writing exercises that follows offers both language arts and non-language arts teachers effective tactics to embed daily, consistent writing assignments into lessons. They are general enough for successful implementation across various subjects, but thoughtful enough to demand higher-level thinking from students.

Teachers appreciate the simplicity of the exercises and the ease with which they can be incorporated into current lesson plans. Students enjoy the reflective nature of the writing assignments. Teachers value that certain writing exercises can double as formative assessments and provide insights into how well each student grasped the lesson. Non-language arts teachers, in particular, like the fact that the exercises are ready-to-use.

Reflective Writing Exercises

Exercise	Why?	How?
#1: Reflect on a Prior Learning Experience	• Memory is enhanced when students understand the connections between prior knowledge and new learning experiences. • Students make meaning out of what they learn when they reflect on prior learning and make connections.	• Students identify three big ideas from the previous lesson. • Students write about why the ideas are important, which idea is most important as it relates to the real world, and which idea interests them the most and why.
#2: Reflect on Visual Stimulus	• Requires students to move beyond simply recalling and describing facts to analyzing and interpreting what they see. • Assists students in developing their ability to empathize with and see different perspectives.	• Choose an image that requires students to organize similarities and differences, trace a sequence of events, discern a point of view, or evaluate an idea. • Give students a bulleted series of questions to guide their writing.

Reflective Writing Exercises (continued)

Exercise	Why?	How?
#3: Reflect on a Reading Assignment	• It is important for students to identify and examine their own thoughts as they read before they can evaluate the words/ideas of others. • Students are able to build a foundation for understanding what they read. • Students are able to make connections.	• Assign frequent writing prompts before, during, and/or after a reading assignment. • Ask questions that encourage students to make connections between the text and themselves.
#4: Reflect on Own Work Ethic and/ or Progress Toward a Goal	• Reveals students' anxieties, mistakes, strengths, and challenges. • Students "reflect forward" to the future as well as back on the past in order to learn about themselves.	• Ask students to reflect upon where they have been and where they are going. • Provide feedback to show support, encouragement, and suggestions.
#5: Reflect on a Historical Event, a Discovery, or a Non-Fictional Incident	• Ask students to think constructively and insightfully about events, experiences, and issues. • Students can evaluate its larger implications by linking the description of the event, experience, or incident.	• Brainstorm key events or an important discovery from the event or incident. • Ask the questions "What happened?" "Who was involved?" "So what?" and "What's next/Now what?"
#6: Reflective Essay Model	• Requires students to not only summarize or describe information, but also assess and evaluate it. • When students can write reflectively about a big-picture question, they demonstrate clarity of knowledge and deep understanding.	• Assign a big picture question. • Students use a graphic organizer to organize their thoughts and information. • Finally, students write their reflective essay.

IL Best Practice 6: Assigning a Curriculum Integration Leader

Primary DSEI Alignment: Instructional Leadership

Element: Integrate literacy, math, and technology across all disciplines

Submitted By: Carol Lopez, Principal, Chambers Hill Elementary School, Harrisburg, Penn.; Glenn Ledet and Doug Walker, Senior Consultants, International Center for Leadership in Education

Summary: Assigning a districtwide curriculum integration leader and strategy to enhance rigorous and relevant learning for all students

Context
There is natural potential for interdisciplinary collaboration between non-core subjects, such as arts and music, and core content subject areas, such as math, science, English language arts, and social sciences. The districtwide initiative to integrate core and non-core subjects, beginning in elementary grades, greatly enhances rigorous and relevant learning for all students.

Overview and Process
All principals in the Central Dauphin School District (CDSD) serve as administrative partners for each of the subject area departments. During a faculty meeting where Carol Lopez, Principal of Chambers Hill Elementary School in the CDSD, was leading her faculty through a lesson-sharing activity, the music teacher shared that he covered some of the same topics and standards being taught by grade-level teachers. Lopez, realizing the importance of integration, asked the District if she could serve as a partner to one of the related arts committees (art, music, PE, and library) in order to implement integration of that subject with the core curriculum. Since all of the creative art departments already had successful administrative partners, the District developed a new leadership partner to promote related arts integration and assigned Mrs. Lopez to this role.

The teachers of the related arts meet monthly; the administrative integration partner meets with these teachers to discuss the advantages of consistent integration and to plan ways to integrate core standards into these classes.

Each group of related arts teachers is given the task of providing a document listing the integrated lessons and skills they provide at each grade level. These lists are reviewed, revised, and approved by the Director of Curriculum and Instruction, and then shared with the other schools in the district.

IL Best Practice 7: Close Reading in the Secondary Classroom

Primary DSEI Alignment: Instructional Leadership

Element: Integrate literacy, math, and technology across all disciplines

Secondary DSEI Alignment: Teaching

Element: Plan and provide learning experiences using effective research-based strategies that are embedded with best practices including the use of technology

Submitted By: Catherine Truitt, Consultant, International Center for Leadership in Education and Andrea Hogentogler, English Teacher, Central Dauphin High School, Harrisburg, Penn.

Summary: A step-by-step process to bring literacy and reading comprehension to every subject

Context

The new Common Core State Standards reflect the belief that literacy is a shared responsibility in schools. *All* subjects—not just English language arts (ELA)—must offer students the chance to engage with rigorous texts in an effort to become critical readers and thinkers. This belief is echoed in the standards themselves: 80–90 percent of the new reading standards require text-dependent analysis. In other words, students must be able to locate textual details in order to cite evidence accurately and engage a text with automaticity.

Regular, structured, and close reading activities across content address the challenge of encouraging this type of reading in non-ELA classes. When implemented throughout a school with fidelity, students experience an intensive analysis of texts that will lead them to literary and intellectual independence.

Overview and Process

The following close reading strategy has been used in the Central Dauphin School District in various subjects with much success since November 2014. (A Close Reading Lesson Planning Sheet and Rubric follow.)

1. The teacher chooses an article that relates, even if loosely, to his or her unit's current topic. The article must be at a high enough Lexile® measure to warrant chunking and rereading.

2. Prior to distributing the article to students, the teacher selects vocabulary to preteach, chunks the text for students, and creates text-dependent questions that increase in complexity as the lesson progresses. A PowerPoint presentation is also useful to help guide the lesson, especially for visual learners.

3. After completing an activating strategy or hook with students, the teacher uses a Frayer model (a four-square graphical organizer used for word analysis and vocabulary development) or some other method to preteach vocabulary.

4. The article is distributed and the teacher reads it aloud. In a class consisting mainly of advanced readers, students read the article to themselves.

5. The teacher asks students to reread the first chunk on their own. Next, the teacher asks the pre-planned text-dependent questions.

6. This process of rereading the pre-chunked text and answering questions continues. Discussion may ensue as the questions increase in complexity.

7. When each chunk has been read twice, the students reread the entire article to themselves.

8. A summary writing assignment (written in the style of a prompt) is given, along with a generic rubric (which follows below). The question must be structured in such a way that it requires students to use evidence from the entire text to answer the prompt.

9. Time and/or student interest permitting, a performance task may be assigned.

Close Reading Lesson Planning Guide

Subject:	Text:

1. Engage students (establish a purpose; "hook" them in; activate prior knowledge):

2. Preteach academic vocabulary (Concept wheel? Word wall? Frayer model?)

3. First read (always the entire text through; teacher reads aloud to students unless students are advanced readers); ask a text-dependent, quad A/recall question:

4. Reread first chunked section; ask a text-dependent, quad A/recall question:

5. Reread second chunked section (be sure your questions are growing in complexity):

6. Reread third chunked section (your questions will now be at an even higher level of complexity and difficulty):

7. Discussion question (use higher-order level questions; i.e., quad C and D verbs):
8. Third read: on own
9. Summary writing assignment (craft a question with specificity):
Performance task (design a task that requires students to apply the information and skills they've learned):

Close Reading Rubric: Summary Writing Assignment

Objective	Emerging 1	Developing 2	Accomplished 3	Exemplary 4	Score
Ideas & Content Main Theme, Supporting Detail	The ideas are unclear, inconsistent, and/or lack a central theme and/or purpose; ideas do not come from the article read during class.	The ideas are somewhat unclear or the attempted development is minimal, too simple, irrelevant, or incomplete; supporting details may or may not come from the article read during class.	The writing is mostly focused, and the reader can easily understand the main idea. Support is present and comes from the article read during class, although it may be too general.	The writing is clear and focused. It holds the reader's attention. Main ideas are developed by supporting details that come from the article read during class and are suitable to audience and purpose.	
Organization Structure, Introduction, Conclusion	Lack of structure; disorganized and hard to follow. Missing or weak introduction and conclusion.	Organization is appropriate, but conventional. Attempt at introduction and conclusion.	Strong order and structure. Inviting introduction and satisfying closure.	Effectively organized in logical and creative manner. Creative and engaging introduction and conclusion.	
Sentence Fluency Rhythm, Flow Variety	Difficult to follow or read aloud. Disjointed, confused, rambling.	Some awkward constructions. Many similar patterns and beginnings. May force the reader to slow down or reread.	Easy flow and rhythm. Good variety in length and structure contributes to the ease of reading aloud.	Sentences are well built, with strong and varied structures that invite oral reading.	

Sample Close Reading Lesson Planning Guide

Subject: World Cultures	Text: http://ideas.ted.com/what-the-best-education-systems-are-doing-right/

1. Engage students (establish a purpose; "hook" them in; activate prior knowledge): If there was one thing that you could change about school, what would it be?

2. Preteach academic vocabulary (Concept wheel? Word wall? Frayer model?) Grit, intrinsic, malleable, antiquated

3. First read (always the entire text through; teacher reads aloud to students unless students are advanced readers); ask a text-dependent, quad A/recall question: According to the text, what is the consequence for South Korea's success with educational reform?

4. Reread first chunked section; ask a text-dependent, quad A/recall question: Why do Koreans place so much emphasis on academic success?

5. Reread second chunked section (be sure your questions are growing in complexity): How is the Finnish model of education different from the Korean model?

6. Reread third chunked section (your questions will now be at an even higher level of complexity and difficulty):

What explanation(s) does the article give for why American schools haven't progressed?

7. Discussion question (use higher-order level questions; i.e., quad C and D verbs):

Predict what the American system of education might look like in five years' time.

8. Third read: on own

9. Summary writing assignment (craft a question with specificity):

What role does the concept of "culture" play in this article's opinion regarding education culture?

Performance task (design a task that requires students to apply the information and skills they've learned):
You have been hired by a new charter school in your town to teach history. But before the school can open, decisions must be made regarding school culture and philosophy of education. Some teachers think the school should be modeled after South Korea's education system, but some favor the Finnish model. You point out that neither is realistic for your town and offer to propose a compromise. Create a sample weekly schedule of a student's typical day at your charter school. Include start and end times, a class schedule and what this student might do during the hours after school until bedtime.

IL Best Practice 8: Measuring Perceptions of Rigor, Relevance, Relationships, and Leadership in a School

Primary DSEI Alignment: Instructional Leadership

Element: Facilitate data-driven decision making to inform instruction

Secondary DSEI Alignment: Organizational Leadership

Element: Create a culture of high academic expectations and positive relationships

Tertiary DSEI Alignment—Teaching Element: Build effective instruction based on rigorous and relevant expectations

Submitted By: Jerry Pedinotti, Vice President, Tipping Point Analytics

Summary: Using surveys to gain insights into how a school's instruction is perceived and make the necessary changes to close the gap between perception and desired learning goals

Context
Feedback from students, staff, and community members can initiate innovative, meaningful school change. When school is an exciting place to be, students are engaged and staff and parents feel empowered to help students reach their goals. By measuring what stakeholders value about learner engagement and the teaching and learning environment, "data" can mean more than results on a test.

WE™ Surveys can provide valuable insight into a school or district's current culture. By gathering baseline data on the perceptions of stakeholders, schools and districts can see where they are, and where they need to be.

Overview and Process
The WE Survey suite is designed to obtain perceptions of ALL students, staff, and community members around the rigor, relevance, relationships, and leadership aspects of a school or district. Feedback from the WE Surveys can initiate meaningful dialogue and innovative

solutions to improve the learning environment for all stakeholders. Parallel items on the student and instructional staff surveys make a comparison of perceptions possible and expose any gaps between the groups. In addition to being very informative and revealing, similarities or discrepancies in perceptions among teachers and students can be unexpected and concerning. In some cases, student and teacher perceptions of their relationships with each other are not always in agreement, and it can be assumed that the work being asked of students had little relevance to the real world.

The survey responses from students, teachers, non-instructional staff, parents, and community can provide the foundation for improvement plans for each of the buildings in the district. Staff from each building can volunteer to be members of a leadership team. These teams work with experienced International Center coaches to review their WE Surveys data and begin to build an improvement plan. As the surveys are completed on a school-by-school basis, improvement plans can be tailored to the needs of each school. School leadership team members are then able to take their training from the coaches and communicate the message and direction of change to the rest of the building staff.

A second administration of the WE Surveys is recommended to allow schools and districts to continue to measure and monitor progress toward alignment of perceptions over time. Each school has its own unique situation. The WE Surveys allow each school to work toward a culture that balances just the right elements of rigor, relevance, relationships, and leadership to benefit all students.

IL Best Practice 9: Student Literacy Growth Profile

Primary DSEI Alignment: Instructional Leadership

Element: Facilitate data-driven decision making to inform instruction

Secondary DSEI Alignment: Instructional Leadership

Element: Integrate literacy, math, and technology across all disciplines

Submitted By: Dr. Patrick Michel, District Superintendent and Chief Operating Officer, Hamilton/Fulton/Montgomery BOCES, Johnstown, N.Y.

Summary: Finding and applying analytics tools that provide truly insightful data that can inform appropriate and productive instructional strategies and interventions as needed

Context

Everyone agrees that reading is important, but the ability of most schools to monitor student literacy levels is marginal at best. A central contributing factor to our ineffectiveness in tracking how well students are doing in reading is that many schools still use norm-referenced data that inform little more than how students are doing in comparison to their peers.

For example, a school may report that a student is reading at 4.2. What does that figure signify? Simply stated, 4.2 indicates what the average reading level is for a group of students that have had four years and two months of reading. In academic terms, it is called the "grade-level equivalent."

In most schools reading is not taught beyond the end of elementary school, except to those students enrolled in remedial reading programs. Therefore, in our secondary schools we often see little growth in student reading levels. Since we use grade-level equivalent scores, however, any particular student may appear to be doing fine in reading as long as the group as a whole does not improve.

Overview and Process

The Literacy Growth Profile, a longitudinal data tool to track and project a student's current and statistically probable future college and career readiness, has helped schools address this challenge. In today's technology-driven, information-based society, the ability to read and understand a wide variety of texts is not only important in academics at all grade levels, but it is also critical in the workplace and in one's personal life.

The Literacy Growth Profile is based on the Lexile® Framework for Reading and tracks the progression of a student's reading ability over time. It can also reveal snapshot data on how prepared the student is to comprehend reading materials from various sources like high school and college level literature and textbooks, military texts, everyday personal use items, and entry-level occupational reading (see graphical example below).

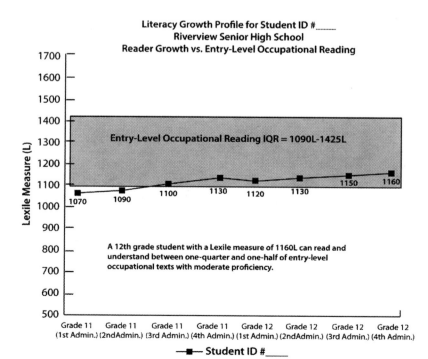

Literacy Growth Profile for Student ID #_____
Riverview Senior High School
Reader Growth vs. Entry-Level Occupational Reading

Unlike grade-level equivalents, the Literacy Growth Profile monitors how well a student is doing compared to the rigorous reading requirements of the new English language arts learning standards, not to other students. This process supports a progression of increasing text complexity so that students can develop and grow their reading skills over time.

The outcome is that students are stretched throughout elementary, middle, and high school and, by the time they graduate, they are able to read at both college AND career ready levels. That, we can all agree, is the "life-level equivalent" for success that really counts.

IL Best Practice 10: Data-in-a-Day

Primary DSEI Alignment: Instructional Leadership

Element: Facilitate data-driven decision making to inform instruction

Submitted By: Pam Boatright, Principal, Truman High School, Independence, Mo.

Summary: A daylong program of classroom observations and student interviews to gather data around a specific topic and apply analysis to a schoolwide improvement plan

Context
"Data-in-a-Day" is designed to provide the building leadership team with data and analysis to inform and support decision making about present and future school improvements. At Truman High School, the program has been extremely effective in modeling and supporting a culture of continuous improvement through purposeful assessment of initiatives.

Overview and Process
Each fall and spring, Truman High School invites a team of its own teachers, as well as teachers and administrators from its feeder middle schools, to participate in its Data-in-a-Day program. The program is planned by a building leader at Truman High School and consists of a daylong series of classroom observations and student interviews.

The focus of the classroom observations and interviews is predetermined by the building leadership team and based on analysis of data collected during the year from various embedded systems of accountability within existing programs. Examples include levels of student engagement and the use of literacy strategies in classrooms.

The following day, participating teachers present their observations and interviews to the school faculty. Each presenter highlights data-supported successes, challenges, and suggestions for improvement. A summative report is then prepared for the building leadership team, which uses the results to create a building improvement plan for the subsequent school year.

IL Best Practice 11: Worlds of Learning @ NMHS: Digital Badges in Professional Learning

Primary DSEI Alignment: Instructional Leadership

Element: Provide opportunities for professional learning, collaboration, and growth focused on high-quality instruction and increased student learning

Submitted By: Laura Fleming, Library Media Tech, Consultant and Creator of Digital Badge PD Platform, New Milford High School, N.J.

Summary: Using a "digital badge" professional learning platform to encourage, recognize, and celebrate continued professional development

Context
Worlds of Learning @ New Milford High School (NMHS) is a digital badge professional learning platform designed to track, share, celebrate and give credit for informal learning. It is NOT a formal teacher evaluation tool. Teachers will be able to take the tools presented in this platform and seamlessly integrate them into meaningful learning that addresses the standards in their respective content areas.

As technology continues to integrate our society and the world in general, it is paramount that teachers possess the skills and behaviors of digital age professionals. Educators should be comfortable teaching, working, and learning in an increasingly connected, global, and digital society. After all, the real aim of educational technology is to modernize pedagogy and to shape the education of the future.

Although the platform was originally created for the staff at NMHS, it has since been opened up for any educator who wants to implement use of digital badges in their school or district.

Overview and Process
The idea behind Worlds of Learning @ NMHS is to provide a platform that provides professional learning with a pinch of gamification. For some time now, digital badges have been used to guide, motivate, document, and validate formal and informal learning. In recent years,

digital badges have evolved from what were originally plain images on a screen to a tool capable of capturing and communicating knowledge. Badges can now contain critical metadata that reflects who issued the badge, who earned the badge, the date upon which it was earned, and any relevant criteria for earning the badge.

Digital badges are flexible enough to be able to recognize the granular skills acquired as well as an individual's total learning. Worlds of Learning @ NMHS was designed in WordPress using a plugin called BadgeOS. The BadgeOS plugin makes it easy to define achievements and organize badge requirements.

The Worlds of Learning @ NMHS platform has been designed so that its resources help educators fully leverage the potential for mastering the digital age skills embodied in the ISTE Standards and the seamless integration of technology addressed in the new state standards.

After registering, teachers can earn badges by learning about a tool and then demonstrating how they have successfully integrated it into their instruction. Teachers must register to access all features of the site. Once teachers begin completing tasks and earning badges, they can then showcase their knowledge by displaying their digital learning badges in various ways:

- By putting them onto Credly, the free web service for issuing, earning, and sharing badges. Credly is a universal way for people to earn and showcase their achievements and badges.
- By putting them on Mozilla OpenBadges Backpack.
- By embedding them into their own sites or blogs and/or pushing them out to their social networks.
- By having their badges showcased on the Worlds of Learning @ NMHS site.

REGISTER/LOG IN   VIEW BADGES   CHOOSE A TASK   EARN A BADGE   SHOWCASE YOUR ACHIEVEMENT

At NMHS, teachers have two or three 48-minute periods per week to engage in growth opportunities of personal interest. During these periods, each staff member creates a Professional Growth Period (PGP) portfolio to present at the end-of-year evaluation conference. The portfolio articulates how the staff member integrated what was learned during this time into professional practice. The badges that teachers earn are a part of their year-long action plan goal.

The platform is available to anyone who feels that digital badges would be a worthwhile tool in their school or district. For more information, go to worlds-of-learning.com.

IL Best Practice 12: Principal Professional Learning Communities

Primary DSEI Alignment: Instructional Leadership

Element: Provide opportunities for professional learning, collaboration, and growth focused on high-quality instruction and increased student learning

Submitted By: Jo-Lynette Crayton, Executive Director for Elementary Schools, Killeen Independent School District, Killeen, Texas

Summary: A plan to ensure principals are included in and feel supported through professional development programs

Context

Teachers commonly participate in professional learning communities, but very rarely do principals have an opportunity to share in "learning sessions" with colleagues. Principals primarily attend meetings where they receive information; they would all benefit by attending more meetings where strategies and tactics to improve both teaching and learning are shared and learned.

Like many districts across the country, Killeen ISD was asking its principals to transition from being building managers to becoming instructional leaders. This shift—from a focus on teaching to a focus on learning—has had profound implications for schools. With increased federal accountability and new, more rigorous standards, district leadership realized that a different approach was needed to create professional development that better connected principals with the curriculum.

Overview and Process

In 2009, the new Superintendent of Killeen ISD reorganized and created the position of Chief Academic Officer (CAO), responsible for school improvement. The CAO's purview included building and overseeing the new Principal Professional Learning Communities (PPLC) program.

After learning goals are determined for the year, a momentum plan is created to identify the appropriate professional development needed to meet district goals. Three Executive Directors, in conjunction with the Assistant Superintendent of Curriculum and Instruction, design learning opportunities for principals.

In Killeen ISD, three meetings are scheduled for each month during the school year, and principals are divided accordingly into groups of six. Each Executive Director facilitates a PPLC and all three PPLCs meet simultaneously. Approximately 95 percent of the learning goals are designed for all staff in the district. Materials are provided and principals replicate the experience on their respective campuses so everyone in the district is following the same plan.

IL Best Practice 13: Focus on Digital Learning Environments

Primary DSEI Alignment: Instructional Leadership

Element: Provide opportunities for professional learning, collaboration, and growth focused on high-quality instruction and increased student learning

Secondary DSEI Alignment: Organizational Leadership

Element: Align organizational structures and systems to the vision

Submitted by: Sheila Mitchell, Superintendent, Anderson County Schools, Lawrenceville, Ky.

Summary: Giving libraries a twenty-first century makeover to accommodate and support digital learning and support technology skill development

Context

We're well aware that too many of our schools are falling rapidly behind these technology-driven times. Many of our schools look like museums serving as record of twentieth-century teaching. One could argue that libraries are the most emblematic relics of twentieth-century learning.

The team at Anderson County Schools in Kentucky decided that libraries were long overdue for a modern makeover. They are transforming their outdated libraries into digital learning centers to provide a central hub for cultivating and reinforcing the technology skills that students will need in careers and life. The welcome change is having the effect of motivating both students *and* staff. The digital centers, and their readily available technology, are enticing and exciting to the school body. They've had an enormously positive impact on fostering collaboration and creativity.

Overview and Process

The Anderson County Schools central office built a "think tank," a room where faculty could go to brainstorm, collaborate, and exchange ideas. The think tank is set up in the style of a modern coffee shop; the idea was to create a relaxed, non-intimidating setting to encourage more free-flowing creative thinking and productive planning.

The library makeover idea was born in the think tank. The middle school was the first school to adopt the concept. They converted the library into a media hub with distinct sections: a book section, which was reduced in size to free up room for other sections; a group meeting section, where students collaborate on projects in a comfortable, coffee shop-style atmosphere; and a creative section, which houses all modern digital devices like 3-D printers, iTVs, iPads, Legos, craft supplies, laptops, and PCs as well as a green wall for recording presentations and student productions. Various types of furniture are organized in different layouts to accommodate all learning styles.

A sample activity of how teachers can creatively use their digital learning environments to expose students to a broad range of technological tools follows. In this particular example, students are asked to read a novel and use various digital resources to indicate their reading comprehension, while also gaining knowledge in how to use and apply these digital resources. Not only is this exercise indicative of the type of learning and creativity that digital learning environments foster, it is also aligned to state standards.

1. Students download the Aurasma app to their digital devices (Anderson County Schools is a bring-your-own-device [BYOD] district). The Aurasma app is an augmented reality platform where you can add engaging digital information to printed material. The app allows students to click on their 3-D creation to upload their Prezi, PowerPoints, and videos. When another student uses their device and scans the 3-D item, they are linked to those Prezi, PowerPoints, and videos.

2. Students read a novel and summarize the plot by creating a storyboard with eight separate events, a 3-D creation that portrays the story's central theme, Prezi or PowerPoint slides, and a presentation video.

On parent night, parents download the Aurasma app to view their child's presentation and the school posts the presentations on their web site.

IL Best Practice 14: Equity Through Family Engagement: The King Project

Primary DSEI Alignment: Instructional Leadership

Element: Engage family and community in the learning process

Secondary DSEI Alignment: Instructional Leadership

Element: Use research and establish the urgent need for change to promote higher academic expectations and positive relationships

Tertiary DSEI Alignment: Organizational Leadership

Element: Create a culture of high academic expectations and positive relationships

Submitted By: Dana Lee, Consultant, International Center for Leadership in Education

Summary: A multi-step action plan to increase meaningful family engagement, particularly with families with two working parents and limited resources, as a proven strategy to improve student achievement

Context

The landscape of American family life changes more with each passing school year. The days when one parent stayed home and was available to support the child at school as needed are less common. Schools today often struggle to find ways to involve and engage families in their children's learning. Many families, especially those that struggle with difficult socioeconomic realities, lack avenues for authentic engagement in their child's education, which is a key predictor of academic success.

Overview and Process

How can schools build on the strengths and capabilities of their students' families and push beyond mere phone calls and conferences that only provide status updates on student progress? Researchers from the Harvard Family Research Project (HFRP), an educational research organization out of Harvard's Graduate School of Education, published a report outlining six steps to engage parents to the end of promoting educational equity and student achievement. The report was named in honor of Dr. Martin Luther King, Jr. as a nod to his legacy vision of a free and just society based on truly equitable opportunities for all. HFRP advises the following six action steps for schools seeking a drastic change in the nature of local family engagement:

1. Underscore how family engagement benefits not just children, but also society at large.
2. Stimulate a social movement that engages parents as a proven tool for high student achievement.
3. Share with families and communities the responsibility to equip children with the technology skills necessary for success in a digital world.
4. Develop policies and plans that connect equitable in-school and out-of-school learning opportunities to reinforce learning and a sense of consistent support.
5. Build inclusive evaluation approaches to reduce privilege and racism.
6. Support ongoing and sustained parent advocacy by cultivating sincere engagement in school events or issues, not mere attendance or passive observation.

Once the decision is made to implement a schoolwide program to address family engagement, teachers and school leaders select those action steps that resonate with their own personal and professional interests. They then subdivide into professional learning communities to tackle the research and literature connected to their action step. These subgroups are given ample time to absorb the material—ideally two to three work sessions with time for processing in between—before being tasked with creating a detailed plan for their particular step.

Between ideas proposed in the literature and those brainstormed by the subgroup, each action step gets fleshed out in a way that's uniquely suited to the local school community. The most impactful action steps are then given even more consideration as the subgroup defines what resources are needed to enact them, including timelines for implementation and benchmarks of success.

The school faculty then gathers to unify their plans. A leader is chosen from each subgroup to brief the others. School leaders guide the discussion as the plans are brought together and refined. Areas of overlap are identified, and so too are areas with gaps. At that point, a schoolwide plan is firmed and adopted, and the work can begin. Subgroups remain responsible for their individual action plans and are checked on periodically to ensure the spirit of the work is alive and thriving.

By empowering choice for each faculty member regarding which arena of family engagement he or she takes on, commitment to the endeavor is strengthened. By breaking into smaller, professional learning communities, the work is more personal and there's more space in which everyone can engage. By leveraging distributed leadership, the burden of enacting a successful family engagement policy is not laid upon the shoulders of the leadership team alone.

Reference

"Promoting educational equity through family engagement: The King legacy." Harvard Family Research Project (14 January 2015). http://www.hfrp.org/family-involvement/publications-resources/ promoting-educational-equity-through-family-engagement-the-king-legacy

Chapter Eleven

Teaching
Best Practices

T Best Practice 1: Developing a Product or Service:
From Concept to Reality

Primary DSEI Alignment: Teaching

Element: Build effective instruction based on rigorous and relevant expectations

Submitted by: Sue Gendron, President, International Center for Leadership in Education

Summary: A real-world, career preparedness project for students to learn the broad range of inputs into launching a business or service, from conducting a market analysis to creating a staffing plan to filling out a two-year financial plan

Context

New state standards caused most states to adopt and incorporate new, more rigorous standards that reflect a more relevant scope of content and relate to the modern world. In each case, the states all claim that their respective revised standards will prepare students to be both college and career ready.

Most school administrators and teachers have a shared sense of what "college ready" means, but there is less consensus on what "career ready" implies. Too often, career ready is equated to career/technical education or "job ready." However, being career ready means having mastered the critical, transferable skills necessary for seamless entry into a future chosen profession.

To address the challenge of preparing students to be career ready, Hilton High School created the Developing a Product or Service: From Concept to Reality initiative for all seniors.

Overview and Process

In this best practice, students take part in a hypothetical new business launch. To begin, students self-select into peer groups of three to five. They then share ideas and conceptualize a product or service for which they believe there would be viable market demand. Students then follow a rigorous process to move from the conceptualization stage all the way to the to-market point. This entails:

- Describing the market analysis they would need to determine the viability of the product or service, including the probable cost of the market analysis.
- Determining and recording the development costs based on the assumption that the market analysis showed the product or service to be feasible.
- Researching and documenting any laws or regulations that could impact the product or service.
- Creating a staffing plan for the development, sale, and support of the product or service.
- Determining the facilities (production and administrative) needed and the cost to purchase, develop, and maintain those facilities.
- Creating a marketing plan and budget.
- Putting together a two-year financial plan using a spreadsheet.

As a final step, the student groups present their product or service as a team to two or three business leaders who have agreed to serve as a review panel.

T Best Practice 2: Early Career Awareness: Linking Lessons to Career Skills

Primary DSEI Alignment: Teaching

Element: Build effective instruction based on rigorous and relevant expectations

Secondary DSEI Alignment: Teaching

Element: Plan and provide learning experiences using effective research-based strategies that are embedded with best practices including the use of technology

Submitted By: Beverly Velloff, Elementary Mathematics Coach, School District of University City, University City, Mo. and Deborah Holmes, Consultant, International Center for Leadership in Education

Summary: Making a habit of always tying a lesson to a real-world application to make learning rigorous, relevant, and engaging to students

Context

Students want to know why they're being taught something. If they do not see a lesson as serving a purpose or having meaning, then they are less likely to engage or enthusiastically attempt to learn the material. If, on the other hand, teachers throughout the system are diligent about reinforcing the long-term goals of each lesson and how they build over time, then students will engage with tenacity. Students who work with a purpose feel like they are building a knowledge base of value that will help them become the people they want to be when older. This instructional practice focuses heavily on engaging all learners by putting content with context. The result is a boost in their confidence and willingness to learn.

Overview and Process

Students benefit when teachers explicitly tie classroom content to the real world. These connections enhance relevance and student engagement. Additionally, students become invested in their learning when teachers link the content to specific careers they could have after graduation. Student confidence and willingness to learn is positively impacted when teachers affirm student work and behavior with comments that recognize possible job opportunities; for example, "You're working like a medical technologist."

During instruction, teachers encourage students to connect classroom content to real-world applications or types of professional careers. A first grade math teacher will *ask* students, "Who am I talking to today?" The students might answer, "Today, I am an engineer," "Today, I am a buyer," or "Today, I am a banker." A fourth grade teacher provides explicit affirmations that make content connections to careers by *telling* students, "You are thinking like an engineer" or "You are thinking like a banker." A seventh grade teacher can *remind* students, "The math you are doing is the kind of work that a sports analyst does" or "Food chemists use this same process."

By asking questions or remarking on the purpose of the learning material, teachers are continuously reinforcing what it takes for students to achieve their long-term goals, whatever they may be. Relevance-based instruction provides students with both a sense of purpose and the tenacity to work harder to reach their full potential.

T Best Practice 3: Creating Real Job Opportunities in the School

Primary DSEI Alignment: Teaching

Element: Build effective instruction based on rigorous and relevant expectations

Submitted By: Sarah Box, Principal, North Side Elementary School, Harrisburg, Penn. and Glenn Ledet, Senior Consultant, International Center for Leadership in Education

Summary: Creating "real job opportunities" to improve student relationships and teach students the responsibility and skills needed to succeed in a career

Context
North Side Elementary School had a traditional student council for many years. After much reflection, it became evident that student council elections were almost always a popularity contest. No matter how much instruction was provided to students about electing a person best suited for the council, it came down to who had the most friends to vote for them. This not only caused hurt feelings, but it also created cliques and divided friendships. There was a need to find a way to improve relationships among students.

Overview and Process
With the district's focus on rigor, relevance, and relationships, North Side Elementary was searching for ways to provide students with meaningful, real-world experiences that increased positive relationships within the building. Sarah Box, Principal at North Side Elementary, instituted a practice that would allow students to experience real-world responsibilities in the form of a job that suited them, while simultaneously fostering relationship building among students.

Students are given an overview of the jobs available to them:

- Actors Guild: Assist in assemblies; create skits to reinforce "High 5 Characteristics"
- WNSE Radio: Assist with morning announcements
- Secretarial Assistant: Work in the office and complete tasks to assist teachers and secretaries
- New Student Guide: Provide a building tour to new students
- Student Mentor: Meet with younger student (similar to Big Brother/Big Sister program)
- Student Buddy: Meet with a younger student each morning to work on academics (sight word cards, read together, work on homework, etc.)
- Safety Patrol: Assist in arrival and dismissal routines, escort students to appropriate spot for pick up, put up the flag each day, etc.

Students choose the jobs they are interested in and complete an application. A staff committee manages these applications and sets up interviews with the applicants. All students who submit applications participate in an interview. After students are interviewed, the staff committee works to match students with an open job. Students then are offered the job and, upon accepting the position, are given training.

This opportunity has made a huge difference at North Side Elementary. The students take their jobs very seriously and there has been an increase in attendance as a result. Even students who traditionally have had poor attendance understand that they have others relying on them to do their job, which provides the incentive to be present. Further, the job program has given many students added purpose. Student relationships, among both student coworkers and student mentors/mentees, have improved. Younger, at-risk students have an older role model to look up to and relationships among students and adults have improved. Students receive support and praise for their work from teachers and administrators.

T Best Practice 4: Who Do We and Don't We Know?

Primary DSEI Alignment: Teaching

Element: Build effective instruction based on rigorous and relevant expectations

Secondary DSEI Alignment: Organizational Leadership

Element: Establish a shared vision and communicate it to all constituent groups

Tertiary DSEI Alignment: Organizational Leadership

Element: Create a culture of high academic expectations and positive relationships

Submitted by: Sue Gendron, President, International Center for Leadership in Education

Summary: A simple tool to identify those students not receiving enough relationship-building attention from teachers and staff, and thus also not receiving a rigorous and relevant education

Context
Some teachers teach subjects. Great teachers teach students. Teachers can reach and teach students most effectively when they know each as individuals and have developed a trusting relationship.

Overview and Process
At East Side Middle School, the principal was concerned that the school had too many students whom the staff did not know well. These students were in danger of falling through the cracks.

Although the staff fully embraces the belief that relevance makes rigor possible, if they don't know their students' interests and aptitudes as well as the challenges and dynamics in their lives, how could they determine what is relevant to them?

To find out how well staff knew the students, the principal had each student's name put on top of a sheet of chart paper taped to the walls around the gym in alphabetical order. The entire staff was then given ten star stickers to place on the ten students they knew best.

Everyone was shocked and dismayed to find that nearly half of the 1,000 students had no stars. The kids who needed us most were the ones we knew the least.

As a result, the school began a whole series of strategic initiatives to get to know all of its students, including their interests and challenges. Tactics included advisor/advisee programs, which carved out time to schedule and conduct personal contact with students and parents via email.

T Best Practice 5: Building Relationships Through Culturally Responsive Activities

Primary DSEI Alignment: Teaching

Element: Build effective instruction based on rigorous and relevant expectations

Secondary DSEI Alignment: Organizational Leadership

Element: Establish a shared vision and communicate it to all constituent groups

Tertiary DSEI Alignment: Organizational Leadership

Element: Create a culture of high academic expectations and positive relationships

Submitted By: Dr. Kathy Attaway, Director of Professional Learning, International Center for Leadership in Education

Summary: Incorporating personal sharing and family customs into learning to build relationships and a sense of community

Context
When kids feel that they are accepted for who they are, they are more likely to be accepting of others. Additionally, students who feel they have good relationships with both their teachers and peers experience a greater sense of belonging in school, which results in greater motivation to become engaged learners.

Overview and Process
Activities that allow students to share information about their families are important in building the relationships that support cultural awareness, respect, tolerance, and understanding. Three elementary-level sample activities to build relationships in an instructionally relevant manner follow.

1. **Star-of-the-Week:** Each week, one child is selected as "Star-of-the-Week." Parents/guardians help the Star-of-the-Week fill out a questionnaire about his or her life, likes, and dislikes. They may also send pictures of the child/family for a Star-of-the-Week bulletin board. In class, the child shares details about his or her life, family, and customs. To enhance discourse and language opportunities, an interview format could be used so other children in the class ask the Star-of-the-Week questions.

2. **Family Treasure Box:** Each child is asked to bring a shoebox containing some of his or her favorite family artifacts. One area of the classroom (e.g., the dramatic play area) is turned into a museum of sorts where the boxes are stored. Each child takes turns playing "museum," complete with advertising, tickets, openings, events, jobs, etc. And of course, each student also "visits" the family treasure box exhibit. Parents of the child whose turn it is to exhibit are invited to participate and be experts. This activity is versatile and can branch off into more possibilities, including having all parents invited at once to make it more of a community event.

3. **Family-of-the-Week:** Each week, invite any or all family members of one student to come and share a family album or a favorite book with the class. This activity highlights the customs and traditions of family life and can facilitate conversations. The family is encouraged to volunteer in the room as much as they can that week. This time provides an opportunity for the family to create a relationship with the teacher and students and contribute to a sense of community. Families that feel welcome and comfortable are more likely to engage in other school or community occasions.

Reference

Dweck, C.S., Walton, G.M., and Cohen, G.L. (2014). "Academic tenacity: Mindsets and skills that promote long-term learning." Paper prepared for the Bill & Melinda Gates Foundation, p. 11.

T Best Practice 6: Flipped Classroom

Primary DSEI Alignment: Teaching

Element: Create and implement an effective learner environment that is engaging and aligned to learner needs

Submitted By: Greg Green, Principal, Clintondale High School, Clintondale Community Schools, Clinton Township, Mich.

Summary: Leveraging technology, students watch instructional videos outside of class and work through assignments in class, allowing the teacher to provide far more hands-on and personalized guidance for each student

Context

In modern society, where technology is ubiquitous and access to information is so readily available, the traditional one-size-fits-all model of education does not provide students with the relevant skill sets to be successful. In the traditional structure, teachers deliver content, typically through lecture, and then students are expected to practice mastery of this content at home. Consequently, the relevance of learning is lost, putting students at risk of disengaging from the process, either by performing poorly on assessments or, worse, dropping out of school completely.

The flipped classroom model inverts traditional teaching methods. Schools that "flip" their classroom use the prevalence of technology to their advantage by having students receive instruction online outside of class and move their "homework" into the classroom. This accomplishes two things: (1) students consume lectures or content at their own pace, and (2) the instructor can use class time to engage ALL students and develop critical analysis and higher-order thinking skills.

Overview and Process

Educational technology and activity-based learning are two key components of a flipped classroom and both influence the learning environment in fundamental ways.

In 2010, Clintondale High School, just north of Detroit, was the first school in the country to become a fully "flipped" model school. Today, students come from all over the metropolitan Detroit area to this School of Choice. (The School of Choice program provides students with additional enrollment opportunities, which range from allowing students to determine which school within the resident district they wish to enroll, to allowing nonresident students to enroll in a district other than their own.) They choose Clintondale High because of the unique support that the school's flipped environment provides.

Prior to 2010, Clintondale High was struggling to educate its high number of at-risk students. Like many schools across the country, Clintondale High was asking its at-risk students to process classroom information in environments that often times are not conducive for learning. The school realized it needed to try a new approach because so many students were failing.

The idea of flipping first occurred to Principal Greg Green when he began recording videos on baseball techniques and posting them on YouTube for his son's team. The recorded content allowed the kids to watch the videos repeatedly to grasp the ideas. This freed up time at practice for more hands-on activity.

This inspired the idea of the flipping concept. Green asked one of the social studies teachers, Andy Scheel, to conduct two classes simultaneously, with identical course material and assignments, and the only difference being that one class was flipped. The flipped class had many students who had already failed the class. After 20 weeks, students in the flipped class began to outperform the students from the traditional classroom model.

Subsequent to this success, teachers throughout the school began assigning instructional videos for homework to be watched online at home (or in the school if students did not have access to the Internet) and began working with students on their "homework" in the classroom.

In 2010, the school used the flipped classroom model with 140 freshman students. The results were immediate and impressive. The failure rate in English language arts was reduced by 33%, by 31% in mathematics, by 22% in science, and by 19% in social studies—*in just one semester*. In addition, there was a two-thirds reduction in total disciplinary issues for freshmen.

How It Works

Two to three times a week, a math teacher, for example, creates or assigns a video detailing several sample problems for students to review and try at home. The school found that shorter videos (three to seven minutes) were better than longer ones because they promoted rewatching. This is especially beneficial to those students who hesitate to speak up or ask questions in class for fear of feeling embarrassed.

When students arrive in class the following day, they form a collaborative learning group with their peers to do labs or interactive activities, applying the skills learned from the video. The teacher circulates the classroom, guiding students through confronting challenges and illustrating concepts per the specific needs of each group. In this model, any problems or questions that a student has are identified and answered by either a classmate or the teacher. Instructors at Clintondale High comment that the flipped approach frees up valuable classroom time to help students master a topic and deepen relationships.

For more information, visit flippedhighschool.com/ourstory.php.

T Best Practice 7: Developing Content Knowledge with Graphs and Charts Across the Curriculum

Primary DSEI Alignment: Teaching

Element: Possess and continue to develop content area knowledge and make it relevant to the learner.

Secondary DSEI Alignment: Instructional Leadership

Element: Integrate literacy, math, and technology across all disciplines

Submitted By: Dr. Susan Szachowicz, Principal (Retired), Brockton High School, Brockton, Mass.; adapted from *Transforming Brockton High School*

Summary: For any new teaching initiative to prove successful, teachers need training and support. Training scripts are a powerful tool for developing content knowledge and skills for analyzing graphs, tables, and charts across the curriculum. It ensures consistent and clear training that results in teachers feeling prepared and confident in applying new instructional strategies and tactics.

Context

To Brockton High School, a school now known for a massive and successful school turnaround and student improvement effort, it became abundantly clear that literacy had to become a schoolwide initiative.

Facing staggering student failure rates, leadership at Brockton had no choice but to get serious about finding a vision to dramatically improve student achievement. Given that a large portion of Brockton's student body speaks a language other than English at home, a focus on literacy became the cornerstone of Brockton's turnaround effort. Literacy—and its four components of reading, writing, speaking, and reasoning—was applied across all subjects and wherever possible with enormous success. In improving literacy, students improved across the board, as literacy empowered them to achieve greater reading comprehension in all subjects.

Overview and Process

Aware that teacher support is integral to implementing any ambitious initiative, through a Restructuring Committee, Brockton developed Literacy Workshops to provide teachers with the depth of knowledge needed to integrate literacy frequently and successfully. The committee developed training scripts as a tool to ensure that all literacy workshops are taught consistently and expertly, and that everyone involved is using a shared vocabulary and has a common focus.

What the committee found was that the training scripts were no small detail; they were the fulcrum on which productive training rests. For teachers to leave a workshop with the depth they needed to effectively apply new strategies and tactics for improved literacy, the training script had to be clearly constructed and effectively used. In other words, a workshop is only as good as its training script.

Over the course of ten years, Brockton became increasingly skilled at deepening the expertise of their faculty in teaching targeted literacy skills, in no small part due to their process of drafting training scripts. In fact, the process is still in practice today. A select group from the committee is charged with preparing a script. From there, scripts are tested on other committee members and select teachers. Scripts are then revised based on reactions and feedback. The process continues until it is evident that a script is complete and capable of informing clear, consistent, and productive workshops.

Brockton used the training script that follows to frame a literacy workshop focused on reasoning skills. This workshop had an ancillary aim of supporting mathematical learning and reasoning.

This workshop begins by teaching faculty the characteristics of line graphs, and then moves into explaining how to model for students a process to analyze, interpret, and create graphs, tables, and charts. Through a series of steps, students are supported as they discern important information, interpret data, draw conclusions, and generate responses. Ultimately, teachers are meant to leave this workshop with a clear plan for how to incorporate this type of reasoning skill and thinking routine across the curriculum.

Faculty Training Script

Analyzing Graphs and Charts Across the Curriculum

Literacy Skills: Reasoning
Lesson Duration: 50 minutes
Link to Standards:

- ELA-Literacy—Integrate and evaluate content presented in diverse media and formats, including visually and quantitatively, as well as in words.
- ELA-Literacy. Reading for Sci/Tech—Translate quantitative or technical information expressed in words in a text into visual form (e.g., a table or chart) and translate information expressed visually or mathematically (e.g., in an equation) into words.

Learning Outcomes: As a result of this training, faculty will be able to:

- Implement the reasoning skills: to create, interpret, and explain a table, chart, or graph; to read, break down, and solve a word problem; to identify a pattern, explain a pattern, and/or make a prediction based on a pattern; to explain the logic of an argument or a solution.
- Implement the reading skill: to understand a concept and construct meaning.
- Model the steps for reading and analyzing and chart or graph for students.
- Instruct their students in the reading and analyzing graphs and charts process using guided practice and independent practice.
- Apply the steps of reading and analyzing charts and graphs to their content area.
- Interpret and evaluate content as it relates to the graphics and charts used.
- Assess students' work using the Graphing Rubric.

I. Introduction

Today's workshop session will focus on helping students analyze graphs and charts across the curriculum. We will work toward using a common vocabulary and process to help students analyze, develop, and apply graphs across all disciplines. Refer to your Graph Vocabulary handout as we explore the process of developing and applying line graphs to solve problems.

II. Teaching the Strategy

Line Graph

Line graphs compare two variables, and each variable is plotted along an axis. Line graphs are useful for showing specific values of data, meaning that given one variable the other can easily be determined.

Point out the parts of the line graph as you review them. *When reading a line graph, carefully review these parts:*

- *Graph title: As with the other types of graphs, the title is usually at the top.*
- *Horizontal axis (or X-Axis): This line on the graph is parallel to the horizon and moves left to right. This line usually represents time.*
- *Vertical axis (or Y-Axis) This line on the graph is perpendicular to the horizon and moves up and down. It usually shows what is happening over time.*
- *Data Point: This point on the graph is where the coordinates of the X and Y axes intersect to provide a piece of data. The data point reflects the relationship between the X and Y axes named by the coordinates.*

Line graphs show trends and changes in data clearly and illustrate how one variable is affected by the other as it increases or decreases. They also allow the viewer to make predictions about the results of data not yet recorded.

Unfortunately, it is possible to alter the way a line graph appears to make data look a certain way. This is done by either not using consistent scales on the axes, meaning that the value in between each point along the axis may not be the same, or by comparing two graphs that use different scales. Be aware that the look of the data on the graph might not be the way the data really is.

Use the following steps when reading a line graph.

- *Step 1: Read the title and write what a graph is describing in your own words.*
- *Step 2: Explain what is being described by each axis, and determine the relationship between axes. Find the label and the unit of measure on the horizontal axis (x-axis) and on the vertical axis (y-axis). If the label or unit of measurement is not apparent, use the information in the title and/or any descriptions provided to determine this information.*
- *Step 3: Mark data points with visible dots. These dots can then be labeled as an ordered pair (x-value, y-value).*
- *Step 4: Create your own questions related to the graph.*

III. Modeling the Strategy

Now that we understand the vocabulary and the four steps in analyzing line graphs, let's go through some examples.

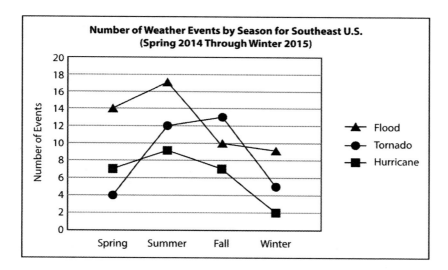

Number of Weather Events by Season for Southeast U.S.
(Spring 2014 Through Winter 2015)

Step 1: *First I read the title and write what the graph is describing. In this case, I may write, "The graph shows the frequency of three dangerous weather events per season for cites in the Southeast U.S. from spring 2014 through winter 2015."*

Step 2: *Then I explain what is being described by each axis by finding the label and the unit of measure on the horizontal axis and vertical axis. For example, I may write, "The horizontal, or x-axis, shows the seasons of the year. The vertical, or y-axis, shows the number of times each event was documented."*

Step 3: Next I identify the data points. The data points are the markers (shapes) within each line. In this graph they signify the mean number of floods (triangle markers), tornados (circle markers), and hurricanes (square markers) in each season.

Step 4: The final step is to create my own questions related to the graph. On an assessment, these may be given to the student. Some examples are as follows:

1. What is the subject of the chart?
2. Which season was the most active in terms of total number of events? The least active?
3. What was the most common weather occurrence in fall?
4. The number of tornadoes in spring was four. What percentage of all spring weather events were tornadoes? What percentage of weather events for the entire year were hurricanes?
5. What conclusion(s) can you reach concerning the most active times for bad weather events compared to the least active times? Do you think the numbers are representative of most years?

Note that questions 1 through 3 start out easy, asking students to identify specific information on the graph. Questions 4 and 5 require students to demonstrate higher-level skills. Question 4 requires students to interpret information and perform calculations. Question 5 asks students to draw conclusions based on the analysis of information from the graph. You could expand this activity by adding questions or having students come up with complex questions that could be presented to the class.

IV. Assessment

Now that we have practiced the four steps, let's use the following example to work through the process in small groups. When you get to Step 4, answer the questions I have posted.

Post the following description, line graph, and questions for teachers to see.

In a few years, you might be interested in getting some kind of part-time job. You find the following line graph, which plots the minimum wage versus time from October 1938 to June 2009. What kinds of things might you be able to tell from it?

The Federal Hourly Minimum Wage Since Its Inception

Source: United States Department of Labor

1. What was the minimum wage in January 1978?
2. When did the minimum wage reach $3.35?
3. In which years did the largest increase in the minimum wage occur?
4. Based on your observations of the graph, make a prediction about what the wage might be in the year 2015.
5. What about the scales used on the graph might make the data appear differently than how it really is?

Allow small groups time to work through the process and then reconvene the whole group to work through any problems or answer any questions.

While we have mostly analyzed graphs today, let's look at an activity that asks students to use their reading comprehension skills, apply their knowledge of graphs to create one of their own, and synthesize information from text and graphs to solve a problem. This type of authentic activity can raise rigor and relevance in our classrooms.

Provide teachers with a copy of the activity. Review the handout together, and answer any questions teachers may have about how graphs have been used in this activity.

Handout

Activity: The Marketing of an Album

Name _____ Date _____

Cost of a Album

Marketing and promotional costs are perhaps the most expensive part of the music business today. They include increasingly expensive video clips, public relations, tour support, marketing campaigns, and promotion to get songs played on the radio. Technology has made it much easier for artists to reach listeners, but it still requires some entity, whether it be a record label or some other representative, to market and promote that artist so that fans are aware that new releases are available.

For every album released in a given year, a marketing strategy is developed to make that album stand out among the other releases that hit the market that year. Art must be designed for the cover and promotional materials (posters, store displays, website graphics, music videos, etc.) must be developed and produced. For many artists, a costly concert tour is essential to promote their recordings.

Another factor commonly overlooked in assessing album prices is assuming that all sales are equally profitable. In fact, the vast majority are never profitable. After production, recording, promotional, and distribution costs, most never sell enough to recover these costs, let alone make a profit. In the end, less than 10 percent are profitable and, in effect, these recordings finance all the rest.

Clearly there are many costs associated with producing an album, and despite these costs, the price of recorded music to consumers has fallen dramatically since compact discs (CDs) were first introduced in 1983. Between 1983 and 1996, the average price of a CD fell by more than 40 percent. Over this same period of time, consumer prices (measured by the Consumer Price Index, or CPI) rose nearly 60 percent. If CD prices had risen at the same rate as consumer prices over this period, the average retail price of a CD in 1996 would have been $33.86 instead of $12.75. While the price of CDs has fallen, the amount of music provided on a typical CD has increased substantially, along with the quality in terms of fidelity, durability, ease of use, and range of extras (e.g., music videos, interviews, and discographies). Content of this type often requires considerable production expense and adds a whole new dimension that goes beyond conventional audio.

In contrast, CD prices are low compared to other forms of entertainment. CDs are one of the few entertainment units to decrease in price, even though production, marketing, and distribution costs have increased.

By all measures, when you consider how long and often people can access the music, CDs truly are an incredible value for the money.

The table below represents retail sales (in millions of dollars):

	2002	2003	2004	2005
Music CDs	803.0	746.0	767.0	705.5

1. Create an appropriate graph below to display the data in the table above. Supply an appropriate title, y-axis label, and x-axis label.
2. From reading the passage above and your own knowledge about music CDs, cite some reasons why sales are projected to decrease.
3. It is estimated that over the last five years, the costs associated with producing a CD have risen 60 percent. If the average price of a music CD was $12.95 five years ago and the costs associated with producing a CD were factored in, what should be the appropriate price of a CD today? Show your work.
4. Discuss the reasons why you think the cost of CDs reflects (or does not reflect) the price you calculated above. Use examples from your graph and/or the reading passage.

V. Summary

Helping our students become more proficient with reading, interpreting, and creating charts and graphs across the curriculum means preparing them for their lives beyond the school walls. Using the four-step process consistently and repeatedly, we can build their confidence in analyzing visuals while also strengthening their problem solving and reasoning skills. Graphs and charts can communicate ideas powerfully in all disciplines and, working together, we can encourage our students to unlock their meaning and potential.

T Best Practice 8: Leveraging Technology to Teach Self-Directed Learning Skills

Primary DSEI Alignment: Teaching

Element: Plan and provide learning experiences using effective research-based strategies that are embedded with best practices including the use of technology

Secondary DSEI Alignment: Teaching

Element: Possess and continue to develop content area knowledge and make it relevant to the learner

Submitted By: Dr. Gregg McGough, English Teacher, Penn Manor High School, Millersville, Penn.

Summary: A selection of digital tactics that empower students to take ownership of their instruction, leverage technology to create self-directed learning, and gain a multitude of online, career-ready skills

Context
Being of a younger, more digital generation, students today have less difficulty in adapting to innovation and change than the instructors who teach them. As digital natives, they are comfortable with constant change and, thus, are generally comfortable with, and motivated by, learning that challenges traditional models by frequent incorporation of technology.

Overview and Process
There is so much work to be done in helping students leverage the Internet for personal growth and learning that there are a multitude of professional development organizations looking for full-time content developers and implementation coaches. I am fortunate to be able to use my experience and doctoral research to work with some professional development organizations to help fellow educators make the transition to 1:1 mobile devices for students, resulting in paperless classrooms that place the power of learning in the hands and heads of students. A few practices I have developed to transition to digital learning follow.

Problem 1: Students receive direct instruction about independent reading assignments during the school day. At some point later that evening—or at a later date altogether—they engage with the assigned text. Since the gap between instruction and student application can be several hours or more, the instructional focus decreases immensely or is lost altogether.

Solution 1: During the assignment stage, my students now use Aurasma, a free app that they access on their mobile devices. Aurasma uses advanced image and pattern recognition that blends texts with rich interactive content (videos or animations) called "auras." As a teacher, I have the ability to insert an aura at specific locations within a text. When a student hovers over a triggering point in the text, a video of me delivering a small lecture appears. This prerecorded video instruction allows students to access direct instruction at the point of learner application. Think of the implications for math or science. Different triggering points could allow students to have a personal tutor on their mobile devices any time, day or night.

Problem 2: My general level seniors still have difficulty with the concepts associated with writing complete sentences. This occurs because they have not taken responsibility for their own instruction or learned to leverage their devices for self-directed learning.

Solution 2: My seniors now take an Edmodo (an online networking application for teachers and students) online assessment, and it scores their responses at the conclusion of the assessment and shows them their gaps in understanding. They then learn how to analyze the results and develop an individual virtual learning plan. The students access Moodle (a virtual course platform) to watch videos on TeacherTube and SchoolTube or to play grammar games aimed specifically at closing the understanding gaps Edmodo revealed. This form of app-smashing (the process of using multiple apps to complete tasks and projects) has allowed my students to take control over their own learning. A recent post-assessment of this exercise showed an average learning gain of 15 percent.

Problem 3: Students sometimes have a difficult time framing claims and providing relevant textual support in the classic rhetorical tradition. During an episode of the podcast *Serial* by Sarah Koenig, I had the idea of teaching my students how to podcast. The difficulty with podcasting is that it can be so technically complicated that the instructional focus shifts toward the tool and away from the actual learning target.

Solution 3: Through my Virtual Community of Practice (VCoP, an online community of experts in a shared field who engage in collective learning and idea exchange) on Twitter, I was directed to an easy podcasting program called *myBrainShark*. This free multimedia tool allows students to narrate a claim, recorded via their mobile devices, and merge it with student-created PDFs that serve as their defense. The program blends visual and auditory elements to result is a stunning demonstration of student multimedia learning. Many of my introverts, in particular, love this method.

T Best Practice 9: Book Buddies

Primary DSEI Alignment: Teaching

Element: Plan and provide learning experiences using effective research-based strategies that are embedded with best practices including the use of technology

Secondary DSEI Alignment: Instructional Leadership

Element: Integrate literacy, math, and technology across all disciplines

Submitted By: Erika Willis, Principal, E.H. Phillips Elementary School, Harrisburg, Penn., and Glenn Ledet, Senior Consultant, International Center for Leadership in Education

Summary: Partnering grade 3–5 students with grade K–2 students in a peer tutoring program to build relationships and improve rigorous and relevant literacy for all students

Context
At E.H. Phillips Elementary School, students are asked to apply reading comprehension strategies to a variety of texts through academic discussions (i.e., listening and speaking) and writing. Teachers attempt to create Quadrant D-level performance tasks to give students the opportunity to experience higher levels of rigor and relevance. One of the ways they have achieved this has been by implementing a peer tutoring program called Book Buddies. The Book Buddies initiative is designed to increase students' reading fluency in activities incorporating higher levels of rigor, relevance, and relationships.

Cross-age peer tutoring has numerous benefits. Both the tutor and the tutee experience the social-emotional benefits of boosted self-confidence and an enhanced sense of belonging in a learning community. Both parties then feel a sense of responsibility to each other which causes both to feel more committed to their own and each other's learning. As an added benefit, teachers gain more time to circulate in the classroom, ensure every student is achieving comprehension, and provide coaching where needed.

Overview and Process

An intermediate class (grades 3–5) is buddied with a primary class (grades K–2) for the year. The students meet weekly or bi-weekly for about 30 minutes. During Book Buddies sessions, students read books together. Older students read in order to practice fluency and model good reading. Younger students read and share books they are interested in to practice fluency. Another option would be for the teacher to read a book aloud to all students and model fluent reading.

After students read or listen to a book, they complete a performance task with their buddy based on the selected theme. The performance task involves a writing component and could involve a presentation component. Here is an example:

- Fourth grade and first grade Book Buddies read *The Gingerbread Man*. For their performance task, students are asked to create a method for trapping the Gingerbread Man. It is required that their work be original (i.e., students design and build their own trap), that they include a written description of their plan, and that they present their trap and plan to the entire group.

T Best Practice 10: Game-Based Learning in the Classroom

Primary DSEI Alignment: Teaching

Element: Plan and provide learning experiences using effective research-based strategies that are embedded with best practices including the use of technology

Secondary DSEI Alignment: Organizational Leadership

Element: Align organizational structures and systems to the vision

Submitted By: Paul Andersen, AP Biology Teacher, Bozeman High School, Bozeman, Mont.

Summary: Using gaming to engage learners, encourage perseverance through failure, and allow teachers to more easily monitor student progress and provide individualized intervention instruction as needed

Context
Students in schools today are "digital natives." They are constantly redefining and expanding the meaning of technological literacy through their regular, daily interactions with technology and digital media. More and more, effective teachers are embracing and incorporating digital media in the classroom as a vehicle to deliver even traditional content.

Paul Andersen, an AP Biology teacher at Bozeman High School in Montana, has created an innovative way to use gaming theory and practices to deliver educational content. His classroom gaming model allows students to be engaged and active thinkers who are motivated to persevere through difficult challenges to attain success, just like in recreational gaming.

Overview and Process
Students, and people in general, are social beings who want to interact with each other. In the traditional, lecture-based classroom model, there is little interaction and students become passive and disengaged. Andersen has taken all of the best and most compelling aspects of video

games and applied them to create an innovative learning experience for his AP Biology students. In his classroom biology game, *Biohazard 5*, students interact in a fun, student-centered learning environment to master high-level biology content. A classroom set of iPads allows students to move independently and watch videos when required.

Andersen believes that our standard education system stigmatizes failure. He is of the mindset that the path to subject mastery will inevitably involve failure, sometimes failing at the lesson many times, and that is OK—it's part of the learning process. If students realize that failure is not a bad thing, but rather a means to success, then they will keep trying until they get it right. In video games, this means "winning."

In *Biohazard 5*, each student starts with zero experience points. As the students achieve mastery in various biology lessons or complete levels, they level-up and accumulate experience points, which are shown on a class leaderboard that the students access from their iPads. The leaders are referred to as "top thinkers," and the board creates a healthy kind of competition in the classroom that further motivates students to improve.

In creating *Biohazard 5*, Andersen produced and posted a collection of videos for his class that follow a complex but highly engaging narrative. He uses various quests and activities that challenge students to think creatively and solve problems. The gaming tool delivers real-time feedback to both students and to Andersen, which gives him the ability to provide individualized attention to students who are lagging and who may require additional instruction.

T Best Practice 11: Technology Integration
Through *Julius Caesar*

Primary DSEI Alignment: Teaching

Element: Plan and provide learning experiences using effective research-based strategies that are embedded with best practices including the use of technology

Secondary DSEI Alignment: Teaching

Element: Create and implement an effective learner environment that is engaging and aligned to learner needs

Tertiary DSEI Alignment: Teaching

Element: Build effective instruction based on rigorous and relevant expectations

Submitted By: Jessica Groff and Joanna Westbrook, ELA Teachers, New Milford High School, New Milford, N.J.

Summary: Merging modern technology and instruction theory with traditional content units to increase rigor and relevance

Context
The principal at New Milford High School asked English language arts faculty members to plan and provide a unique learning experience around traditional content units using effective, research-based strategies and best practices. The faculty members opted for the best practice of integrating technology into a unit to increase levels of student engagement, rigor, and relevance.

Overview and Process
Jessica Groff and Joanna Westbrook, team members in the English department, conceptualized and developed a lesson that incorporated the relevant use of social media into the traditional unit on Shakespeare. Students were asked to use Twitter to build on and engage in content authentic to the play *Julius Caesar*.

To accomplish their goal of creating a rigorous, relevant, and technology-based lesson plan for a traditionally nontechnological unit, the teachers began by researching the history of the Roman Forum. This was a critical step to ensure that the ensuing discourse via social media was within a relevant historical context and the boundaries of the academic content that needed to be covered.

The teachers guided students through an observational exercise to deconstruct the typical tweet. From there, everyone collaborated to generate a list of example tweets that were representative of the standard format so that students would feel comfortable drafting a tweet on their own. Teachers also instructed students on how to use Mozilla Thimble to create memes—items in the form of an image, video, phrase, etc., that spread via the Internet within and/or across cultures or groups of people—to allow students with varying degrees of tech experience to present their visuals in a more professional manner.

The integration of technology in the Shakespeare unit made it possible for students and faculty to approach language arts lessons in a fresh way while also raising levels of rigor and relevance. Students have shown an increasing level of content interest and engagement because of the required incorporation of digital media to complete assignments. The use of Twitter and Mozilla Thimble has brought visual clarity, humor, and creativity to students' learning experiences.

T Best Practice 12: Formative Assessment: The Exit Ticket

Primary DSEI Alignment: Teaching

Element: Use assessment and data to guide and differentiate instruction

Submitted by: Teresa L. Glavin, Instructional Support Services Director, Otsego Northern Catskills (ONC) BOCES, Grand Gorge, N.Y.

Summary: A quick, simple, end-of-class-session assessment to ascertain the level of classroom-wide comprehension and inform the instructional agenda for the next session

Context
One-time, high-stakes state assessments are neither an efficient nor effective way of measuring student knowledge or content mastery. Schools and districts must transition to a process of frequently assessing students in class to get a clearer picture of individual learning. Effective teaching and learning does not happen when the same few students raise their hands; teachers must have some form of regular assessment that indicates classroomwide comprehension.

Formative assessments engage all students and provide critical evidence of student learning, which helps inform instruction.

Overview and Process
The Exit Ticket is a formative assessment technique that is used prior to class dismissal and provides immediate and informative evidence of student mastery of lesson content. It is a very simple strategy that costs little to nothing and takes barely a minute to conduct.

At the close of each lesson, I ask all students to write on an index card a simple but informative response to a higher-order question that I develop specifically to reveal evidence of understanding. Depending on what the lesson warrants, students may be asked to write down something such as an important concept they learned, a relevant takeaway, an unresolved question, a prediction of what might transpire next, a simple application or solution to a problem, or a simple response to a prompt.

The quick responses that Exit Tickets provide are extremely helpful for teachers when planning the next day's instruction. Teachers gain understanding of who knows what and if certain topics need additional instruction time or clarification. This end-of-class reflection by each student helps solidify learning before moving on to the next class or activity. It is also an opportunity for students to ask for help or further explanation.

There are times when similarly answered Exit Tickets will indicate that a group of students share the same difficulty grasping a lesson. Flexible reteaching groups can then be organized with students grouped into teams by similar misunderstanding. Where possible, a student who has indicated content mastery can function as a tutor for groups needing additional learning. This can be an empowering learning strategy and gives students different perspectives on possible solutions. It also frees the teacher to monitor and facilitate learning as needed.

T Best Practice 13: Electronic Portfolio of Student Work

Primary DSEI Alignment: Teaching

Element: Use assessment and data to guide and differentiate instruction

Submitted By: Dr. Michael Nagler, Superintendent of Schools, Mineola Union Free School District, Mineola, N.Y.

Summary: Using app technology to generate student portfolios, which enable simple and swift progress tracking and insights for differentiated instruction

Context

The implementation of new rigorous and relevant standards for students requires new assessments that properly measure student growth in those standards. Too many school districts lack a grading infrastructure that supports standard-based grading.

Overview and Process

We are beginning to see an emerging trend that moves away from traditional grading (as in a curriculum) to one that measures student performance through demonstration of mastery on specific standards. Mineola Union Free School District (UFSD) entered into a collaborative partnership with educational app and technology content creator School 4 One to build an app that creates an e-portfolio of student work to capture student progress within the standards. The app makes it easier for teachers to see what students know and, more importantly, it provides real-time actionable data on what students don't know.

Mineola UFSD partnered with the School 4 One creators for six months under a no-cost agreement to develop the app to the specifications of the district. The app was made available to every student in grades 3–7, totaling approximately 1,100 kids. All New York State English and math modules were embedded in the app for those grades to become a fully customized Web portal where teachers could import and present instructional videos. In the videos, the instructor records himself or herself introducing the lesson. Graphics and effects are blended into the clip to enliven and supplement the lesson. At various points during the video, the instructor asks questions of the student, either open-ended (such as a formula) or multiple choice, for which the student must type in an answer.

All materials are presented through the app in the form of standards-based assignments, which students can access and work on directly through their iPads. Each lesson, standard exercise, and unit is stored in the app and amounts to what is a portfolio of each student's work and, thus, performance over time.

Upon completion of an assignment, the work is digitally transmitted back to the instructor. At this point, the teacher has options about what to do with the submitted student work. Through the app interface, he or she can type in feedback, draw a checkmark, or click a record button to provide verbal feedback to the student. At the bottom of each submitted work, there is a four-point rubric—tied to the state standard—where the teacher can give a score. That score is automatically uploaded and recorded in a digital grade book.

The grade book is an extremely powerful tool that instructors can use to review and analyze data in a number of ways to provide insight into how students are progressing individually and as a class. In turn, teachers can determine where and how differentiated instruction is needed. On the grade book screen, students are listed in rows and all of the assignments are shown in the column headers. How a student performed on any given assignment is shown in a color-coded cell where the two meet. The app has the functionality to switch out the assignments for the actual state standard that the assignments assess. The app shows how many times the standards were assessed during the year and what the most recent score for each student was on them.

Through the app, teachers can view a student's scores for all assignments that pertain to a particular standard. This ability to view standard-specific composite data provides a picture of how that student has progressed over time relative to that standard. The teacher can determine if there has been growth toward mastery or if the student is struggling to comprehend and apply the material.

The app can also provide the teacher with a class-level report of all students' performance on a standard. If a certain standard is giving a large number of students in a class trouble, the instructor can identify and select a lesson that is differentiated to accommodate those students that require the most remediation. For example, the teacher can create and assign additional videos for students to watch. This use of Automated Data-Driven Instruction is embedded in every teacher's grade book as they create their lessons. We are also working on merging the metadata generated from these videos with the School 4 One portfolio data.

T Best Practice 14: Focused Differentiated Instruction

Primary DSEI Alignment: Teaching

Element: Use assessment and data to guide and differentiate instruction

Secondary DSEI Alignment: Teaching

Element: Further content and instructional knowledge through continuous professional learning that is both enriching and collaborative

Submitted By: Andy Bristow, Principal and Marcie Donaldson, 7th grade Reading and Language Arts Teacher, Simpson Middle School, Cobb County School District, Marietta, Ga.

Summary: Incorporating differentiated instruction tactics in content, process, and product through learning style, readiness, and interest provides learners with the appropriate challenge to stretch toward their potential

Context

When teachers incorporate best practices into the classroom, students become more motivated to take ownership of their learning. At Simpson Middle School (SMS), we give all students the opportunity to participate in Advance Content (AC) courses. In the past, only students identified as gifted were allowed to take AC courses. Today, our goal is for all students to take at least one AC course during their three years at SMS.

Eighty-three percent of SMS students are currently enrolled in at least one AC course, compared to as few as 20 percent of their peers enrolled in AC courses at neighboring schools with similar demographics. In addition, over the past five years, every core teacher has been trained in strategies for AC instruction and has acquired Gifted Endorsement.

Overview and Process

When we set the goal for all SMS students to take at least one AC class, we realized we needed more tools to differentiate instruction so that each student could improve to the point of qualifying for an AC class.

With new high expectations for all students, all teachers had to enhance their ability to teach effectively to a student base diverse in ability, background, and needs. Two examples of differentiated instruction best practices, with which we've had great success, follow.

Bringing the Holocaust to life using *The Boy on the Wooden Box: How the Impossible Became Possible . . . on Schindler's List* **by Leon Leyson**

With new national standards, students are expected to read at a higher level. As an exercise in advanced reading, my class read *The Boy on the Wooden Box: How the Impossible Became Possible . . . on Schindler's List* by Leon Leyson. The memoir describes Leyson's experiences from the 1930s, when Nazis invaded his native country of Poland, through the 1990s and his life in his adopted country of the United States.

The Lexile® level for this book is 1000L. (A Lexile® measure provides insight into either an individual's reading ability or the difficulty of a text. The Lexile® measure is shown as a number with an *L* after it: 880L is 880 Lexile®.) My students read between 685L and 1145L and range from the 14th percentile to the 99th percentile on the IOWA reading assessment.

In order for all students to understand this book completely, the instruction needed to incorporate some scaffolding. An English Language Learner student had the opportunity to listen to a portion of the book on tape, while other students read it independently. Some students had complex organizers with multi-facets, while others had basic organizers with fewer facets. Open-ended questions were provided at different levels of Bloom's Taxonomy. Vocabulary was pre-taught in a variety of ways to appeal to students' learning styles.

After reading the book, students completed a Web Hunt—an inquiry-oriented lesson format in which most or all the information that learners work with comes from the Web. The Web Hunt was focused on gathering information from before, during, and after the Holocaust. The process of gathering material was differentiated based on students' preferred learning modality; they were able to make choices around the difficulty level of reading materials, examining pictures, and/or watching video clips.

After collecting background material, students participated in a multiple intelligence exercise and they were to work as though in partnership with a local museum. The students had certain standards they had to meet as though they were being commissioned by the museum to help create a display to honor Leyson. Students synthesized the information from their research and the memoir to create a display showing Leon's life before, during, and after the Holocaust. Each student also partook in a performance that analyzed the difficulties of life during this time period and examined the impact of humanity during Leyson's experience. Students were encouraged to perform in a way that was comfortable to them:

- Theatrically inclined students wrote and performed monologues.
- Several students who were interpersonally inclined created movies.
- A couple of naturalists compiled a photo gallery and blog.
- A musical student wrote her own music, played it on her flute, and put her music to pictures.
- Mathematically oriented students built timelines.
- Spatially oriented students made or used a 3-D printer to design and print sculptures.

Understanding a leader's vision using *Long Walk to Freedom: The Autobiography of Nelson Mandela* by Nelson Mandela

Another group of students read Nelson Mandela's autobiography, *Long Walk to Freedom*. This project was rich in activities for students:

- Throughout the process of reading the book, students chose the form(s) of expression with which they were most comfortable, e.g., journals, letters, pictures, tableaus, poems, discussions, and presentations, to demonstrate their reading progress and comprehension.
- Once all students had completed reading the book, each participated in a QR code hunt. The QR code took the students to websites that presented various resources such as music,

movie clips, charts and diagrams, pictures, poems, definitions, and articles. At each website the students had to respond to a high-level open response question. After students finished the QR hunt, they were put into groups of four where they participated in a silent discussion. Each person had a different question that required a thoughtful answer. Students responded, passed the paper to the next student, who added to the previous group member's response until each question was viewed and answered by all four members.

- As a classwide empathy-building exercise, we reconstructed Mandela's jail cell to scale so students could grasp the small dimensions in which he had to live for nearly thirty years.
- As a culminating activity, students came up with a metaphorical expression to capture their reaction to the book and then presented it to the class. The following were criteria that students had to use in completing the assignment/performance task:
  o Comparing Nelson Mandela's leadership to another object.
  o Drawing conclusions, inferring and making comparisons using nonlinguistic representation.
  o Working in small groups of two to three, some students wrote an expanded summary of their comparisons.

This performance task allowed students to show their understanding of Nelson Mandela's devoted mission to liberate the oppressed and the oppressor to advance freedom for all.

The following table is a sampling of activities to bring differentiated instruction to your classroom. It shows how differentiated instruction tactics may be integrated throughout a lesson to foster students' enthusiasm while developing their critical and creative thinking skills.

Teaching Goal	Practical Activities
Introduction of skills or concepts	• Students view video clips and photos that introduce them to time period of the stories. • Students complete research tasks to practice information-gathering skills and gain contextualized knowledge of the topic at hand. • Students engage in historically relevant and appropriate reenactments as an empathy-building exercise.

Assessment of individual student learning	• Quick formative assessments:
	  ○ Tickets out the door
	  ○ Thumbs up, thumbs down
	  ○ Quick writing prompts
	  ○ Socratic method
	  ○ Journals
	  ○ Silent discussions to assess student learning
	NOTE: Performance tasks serve as summative assessments.

Real-world applications of acquired skills	• Students write journals about their experiences. • Students create tableaus documenting different activities around story subjects. • Students develop a real-life scenario of the characters' environment and participate in the scene through a performance exercise (which can serve as a summative assessment).

T Best Practice 15: Literacy Workshops to Improve Literacy Across Subjects

Primary DSEI Alignment: Teaching

Element: Further content and instructional knowledge through continuous professional learning that is both enriching and collaborative

Secondary DSEI Alignment: Instructional Leadership

Element: Integrate literacy, math, and technology across all disciplines

Submitted By: Dr. Susan Szachowicz, Principal (Retired), Brockton High School, Brockton, Mass.; adapted from *Transforming Brockton High School*

Summary: Professional learning workshops on teaching targeted literacy skills resulting in improved student performance across subjects

Context
Brockton High School, near Boston, Mass., has been one of the nation's most rapidly improving schools since the early 2000s. This was certainly not always the case at Brockton; by the late 1990s, 44 percent of its 10th graders were failing English, and 75 percent were failing math. Leadership knew they had no choice but to figure out how to turn things around and fast. First, they cultivated a culture of respect and responsibility between and among adults and students, which grew into the foundation for great academic achievement. Second, they formed a Restructuring Committee of key faculty and staff with two goals in mind: improving student academic achievement and personalizing the educational experience for all students.

As they charted a path to rapid school improvement, the committee had challenging demographic circumstances through which they had to navigate:

- 76 percent minority
- 50 different languages spoken
- 40 percent speak a language other than English at home
- approximately 17 percent in Transitional Bilingual Education

As the committee looked at assessment data, one thing became abundantly clear: all teachers needed to commit to teaching literacy across subjects. Given that language was such a major obstacle at Brockton, this felt doubly crucial and urgent.

Overview and Process

How was Brockton going to equip its faculty to teach literacy wherever and whenever possible? The Restructuring Committee came up with the idea of Literacy Workshops, where members of the faculty would be appointed to guide teachers through a systematic and results-driven approach to teach a certain literacy skill. The Literacy Workshops were part of a larger professional development program to provide teachers the skills, resources, and support they needed in applying an array of new instructional strategies and tactics aimed at boosting achievement for all students. The Literacy Workshops were of particular importance because by improving literacy skills, students would gain the reading comprehension and language skills to improve in all subjects.

While an individual workshop would hone in on one literacy skill, as a series, all areas of literacy would eventually be addressed: reading, writing, speaking, and reasoning. To amplify the impact of the workshops and also account for their efficacy, the committee collaborated to put them within a broader and strategic framework.

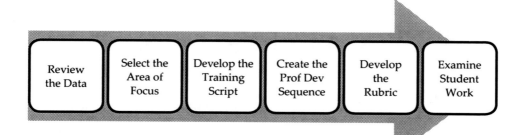

To begin, the Restructuring Committee collaboratively reviews student performance data to determine areas where students are having difficulty or where there seem to be gaps in instruction. From there, the committee can ascertain professional learning needs and, in particular, where teachers appear to need a literacy workshop. Once the committee has settled on the specific literacy skill on which the next workshop will focus, certain committee members begin writing the training script. The training script is then tested with other members and select teachers. It is refined based on feedback. This process continues until the script has proven capable of serving as the guide for a productive professional learning experience with the entire staff.

From there, the committee develops the sequence of the workshop. In the workshop, it is made clear that all teachers are required to use the strategy the same exact way, and they are given an implementation schedule. The committee develops a common scoring rubric to set clear expectations for students in their demonstration of mastery over the skills that are the focus of any given literacy workshops. From there, implementation begins, following the schedule developed by the implementation team. Finally, as teachers begin to see improvements in student literacy skills, outcomes are acknowledged and celebrated, not only for students but teachers as well.

Epilogue

Willard R. Daggett in His Own Words

Willard R. Daggett has spent his entire career in education, first as a teacher, administrator, and coach, then as a state administrator, and finally as the founder and chairman of the International Center for Leadership in Education, based in Rexford, N.Y. Writer Tim Weller interviewed Bill for these closing thoughts.

How did you develop the Daggett System for Effective Instruction?

Our unique signature as a company came out of my own belief that, given the right conditions, all kids can learn. But they can't all learn at the same rate, and you can't use the same strategies for all students. If you go way back to my early years in teaching, I was the one who got the kids that everyone else had given up on. I liked those kids a lot! They were good kids, but they weren't good students. And one of the reasons for this was that the system had beaten them down over the years. They weren't good at traditional academics, but they were smart kids. They had practical experience because they had become savvy, which was almost like a survival mode when they were growing up.

So I used different approaches on a trial-and-error basis and developed some best practices that worked for these kids. I also began to network with some other educators who thought the way I did.

Together, we really developed some pretty successful and unique strategies, the most basic being that relevance makes rigor possible. If you make instruction relevant to kids and get them engaged, they'll do better in school.

But as the business grew, I knew I couldn't just keep doing what I was doing based on a best practice here or there. I began to see what a lot of other educators were talking about, which was this: yes, instruction had to be strong, but in addition—and this is important—you had to have strong leadership in the building. The phrase "principal as an instructional leader" became important. Historically, principals were like clerks of the works—they made sure the building was opened and closed, that there were no fights, and that the bus and athletic schedules ran smoothly. But they did not have responsibility for setting up and developing practices to help teachers become successful. I understood that it was more than strong teachers or strong teaching practices; it was also what the principal does. You have to set up a structure where improving student performance is valued and supported at the building level. I wasn't alone in this; there were three or four of us around the country who saw this. Fortunately, this simple, common sense belief started to catch on.

By the mid-1990s, everyone was using the term "principal as instructional leader." If you look at our system, we had developed two of DSEI's three components: teaching and instructional leadership. The third and final element was informed by a major grant awarded to the International Center by the Bill & Melinda Gates Foundation. We partnered with the Council of State School Officers and went out around the country to find the nation's most rapidly improving elementary, middle, and high schools. At each of these schools, we dug deep and went below the surface. This is what we found: yes, strong teaching practices are important, and yes, the principal as instructional leader was important. But we also discovered that central administration played an important role as well. Central administration had to be purposeful in their selection, support, and evaluation of their principals. Central administration had to create a strong vision—that all students can and will learn—and then create core strategies to make that happen.

We called that organizational leadership, and that was the final segment of DSEI.

So what happens when a district reaches out to you for help?

The first thing we do is come in and help them create a plan, which involves situational analysis and strategic planning to tailor our approach to a school's or district's specific needs. Our approach here is collaborative, not evaluative. That's extremely important to understand. We're not here to judge and tell a school or district whether they are doing a good or bad job. We're not going to come in and tell them *what to do*. What we do is ask them a lot of tough questions and try and guide them to come up with their own answers. I keep using this sentence over and over, but it's true: *culture trumps strategy.* If you don't own the process and the solution, the minute my staff leaves your district, the solution falls apart. They've got to own it! That's why we call our approach collaborative.

Next, we help the district build a culture. We help create a systemwide approach to teacher support. We work with them to help create instructional effectiveness and provide tools to increase rigorous learning for ALL students. We help them establish a clear focus and teach them how to take action through data.

From there, we provide shoulder-to-shoulder coaching to prepare leaders to accurately observe classrooms for indicators of instructional excellence. Then we follow up with ongoing coaching to ensure continued progress and consistent practices.

What's important here is that no single approach works for everyone. Every school district has its own DNA, and until you understand what that DNA is, you won't be able to come up with a viable solution. A good analogy would be building a house. You know you need a good foundation. You know you need electricity and water, but how you put it all together varies based upon the needs and interests of the homeowner and the size of the property. You're not going to create the same blueprint for every house. Schools are the same way.

Do you worry that DSEI might become obsolete at some point in the future because of our rapidly changing technology?

No, I don't think DSEI will become less effective in the future. Teaching, instructional leadership, and organizational leadership will remain cornerstones. But I do think that the practices within each DSEI segment will constantly change. What was a good practice three years ago, especially if it involved instruction, may not work today because it's been dramatically impacted by technology. That is why we continue to find, refine, and share innovative best practices on an ongoing basis.

One final point about DSEI. What happens in most school districts is that information and communication flow from the top down. That's how most decisions are made. We believe that's incorrect. We think information and communication should start at the teaching level and flow up to the instructional level. We think decisions at that level are best informed by teaching. Teaching should not be depressed by instructional leadership. Superintendents and principals should be empowering teachers so they can build relationships and increase student achievement. Unfortunately, in many districts, there are more and more obstacles put in teachers' way. Superintendents and principals need to figure out how they can remove these obstacles or work around those they can't so the decks are cleared for teachers to do what's best for students.